A Glimpse of the Sunshine

GRIPPED BY PAIN
AND DESPAIR,
HER LIFE BECAME
A SLOW
AND QUIET
MIRACLE

EDITH A. REUSS

Tyndale House
Publishers, Inc.
Wheaton, Illinois

All Scripture quotations in
this book are from *The
Living Bible Paraphrased.*

Library of Congress Catalog
Card Number 78-57961
ISBN 0-8423-1036-3, paper.

First printing, March 1979.
Printed in the United States
of America.

To my friend Ro, who believed in me

ONE

Systemic lupus erythematosis. An ugly and frustrating disease. No known cause. No known cure. Certainly not a diagnosis you'd associate with joy and thankfulness.

But our God is strange and wonderful. He does miraculous things. He can turn hopelessness into confidence. He can turn pain and despair into strength. He can turn something as ugly as my lupus into a source of beauty.

I'd always sought joy in my life, but not until I found out that I have lupus did I learn what real joy is. It's been a slow and quiet miracle. And it's still unfolding.

What is the joyful, contented life? I ached for it as long ago as I can remember. As a child I thought it would come when I went away to college and became independent. When I met Tom and fell in love, I thought it would be when we were married. When he was in the seminary and we struggled financially, I thought it would come with his first parish. The present was never good enough; the future held everything.

Tom was finally ordained in 1971. How excited we both were! When he accepted his first call and we moved to the tiny town of Miller, Iowa, life seemed brimful of every imaginable blessing.

I had a husband I both loved and deeply respected. I was

confident in his wholehearted love for me. Our two sons
were normal and happy. Jonathan was two and a half, bright,
extremely active. Six-month-old Peter was a cuddly redhead.

Miller was a great place to raise young children.
Unincorporated, it boasted nothing more than a handful of
homes, a feedstore, and the church. The front windows of the
parsonage looked out at a chicken farm. And we could see
acres of beans and corn stretching out to the horizon from
the back.

The parsonage itself was a huge old farmhouse, a vast
relief from the cramped trailer of our seminary days. The
rooms were sunny—and newly paneled and papered. And
there were just enough quirks to give the place a personality
of its own. I immediately fell in love with that old house.

The yard rambled on and on. Tom promptly planted a
huge garden. We even had an everbearing strawberry bed
that allowed us to indulge in berries morning, noon, and
night. In that setting we could spread out both literally and
figuratively.

The congregation itself was kind and responsive to Tom's
ministry. They brought me eggs and brownies. They offered
advice on toilet training and jelly-making. They made us feel
truly accepted.

It was the kind of life I'd always dreamed of. Now I'd
arrived at the end of the rainbow. But to my astonishment,
there was no pot of gold. Instead I found in myself only a
growing resentment and a frightening aloneness.

Resentment? I resented everyone and everything.

Tom loved being a pastor. After years of preparation he
was finally doing the work he wanted, and he discovered that
he was really good at it. I remember one day when he came
home from church whistling and dancing. "It just doesn't
seem fair to get paid for something I enjoy doing so much,"
he said with a happy grin.

Instead of rejoicing with him, I was filled with heaviness.

He went to church each morning and had uninterrupted time
to write his sermons and plan his classes; *I* dusted and cleaned

toilets with constant time-outs for wet diapers and spilled milk. *He* had leisurely visits with the parishioners and was even doing some counseling; *I* had only Jonathan and Peter for company. Even when I coffeed with a neighbor, the conversation never seemed to get beyond kids and recipes. Tom was free; I was trapped.

Women's liberation was just getting my attention at that time. I firmly believed that a mother with two babies belonged in the home; I never really considered getting an outside job. Yet I was aware that my own set of talents and abilities had little to do with housekeeping. Certainly I had more to offer the world than knowing which detergent worked best in Miller's hard water! My job as a full-time wife and mother seemed so mechanical.

Magazine articles screamed out at me that I should learn to be creative in my homemaking; *then* I would find satisfaction. So I baked my own bread and canned and fingerpainted with Jon. I tried to keep my home like a picture from *Better Homes and Gardens.* But the pictures in that magazine were never enhanced with Cheerios ground into the kitchen floor or toy blocks tumbled on the sofa. Every morning I bravely made a list of all the things I would accomplish that day, but by evening I was seldom more than halfway through my list. Constantly I despaired that homemaking was the only thing I was doing, and I was doing a lousy job at it.

One afternoon I wailed to Tom as I looked at the newspapers strewn on the floor and the dirty dishes piled in the sink. "My whole purpose in life is to keep this place clean, and just look at it!"

"Is that your purpose in life?" he asked quietly.

I burst into tears.

I was resenting Tom's work as much as his satisfaction in it. I'd looked forward to long cozy evenings together after the boys were bedded down. No more seminary papers hanging over his head! But now he had meetings instead of papers, and I spent long evenings alone.

I resented the subtle and not so subtle pressures exerted to mold me into a "good" pastor's wife. I truly enjoyed giving devotions and occasionally leading Bible studies, but I didn't want to be railroaded into it. I felt a loss of integrity at shaping my own place in the church and community. Everything was assumed for me.

More than anything I resented the boys' constant demands on my time and energy. I wanted time to think and dream and create, and I couldn't even take a bath without interruption. They never seemed to nap together. Jon followed me constantly, "helping" and demanding that I read to him. Since I was nursing Peter, I was physically chained to his needs. By the time I got them both to bed at night I was drained.

Tom offered me an hour every day after lunch to hole up in my sewing room and do as I liked. Those sixty minutes seemed so precious that I couldn't bear wasting them. I drove myself from one project to another until I found myself coming out of my break more exhausted than before.

I had always dreamed of having a daughter and had found it hard to hide my disappointment when Peter was born. The disappointment lasted. It dug deep into me. Somehow a daughter seemed the key to contentment. So I nagged at Tom until he finally agreed to my pleas to adopt a girl.

We made a preliminary application with an agency that handled Korean children. Yet even in the excitement of planning her room and daydreaming about her arrival I felt fear. I wondered if I could handle three toddlers. I wondered if this bid for contentment would lead to another dead end. I couldn't admit my fears even to Tom. Getting a daughter seemed the only chance I had.

Aloneness. I knew no one to whom I felt I could confide my feelings of resentment, guilt, fear. It was as if I were in a self-made prison with walls that kept getting higher and higher. I saw no escape.

The diapers piled up. The boys cried in the summer heat. Vegetables ripe from the garden demanded immediate attention. And I was so tired! I woke up tired each morning. I rested during any rare minutes in which both boys were down; I even went to bed early. Sleep seemed my only way out. How I hated the sound of the alarm! I could even explain my tiredness in psychological terms: it was an evasion of my problems. So I felt guilty about being tired.

At first Tom could bring me out of the whirlwind of my feelings with a quiet evening together or an unexpected hot fudge sundae. We were confident that they were "new baby blues"; that my strength would return and so would my spirits. But I got worse instead of better. Fear for my sanity turned into hopeless anger. I lashed out bitterly against Tom.

One afternoon we sat at the kitchen table, Peter sleeping and Jon playing quietly in the next room. As we drank tea Tom allowed me to spill out all my bitterness and frustration. When I finally finished there was a long and uncomfortable silence. Then he said softly and hesitantly, "I think you should see a psychiatrist."

My reaction was typical, I think. I burst into tears. Even Tom didn't understand! I was a college social work major. I knew all about Freud and Eric Erickson and how to handle feelings. A psychiatrist couldn't help.

Tom suggested that we pray together, but I had long ago stopped praying. God seemed so remote, so uncaring. I wasn't even sure he was there.

Soon after that I caught a cold. At first I ignored it, but it turned into a severe sinus infection and I reluctantly went to the doctor. I remember making a wry comment on the way home about my fifteen-dollar sniffles.

The cold was followed by a strange burning rash all over my body. "Nervous eczema," said the doctor. He prescribed medication and the rash seemed to go away.

The rash was followed by severe cramping sensations. "Nervous stomach," said the same doctor. More medication.

The cramping was gradually replaced by aching in my

joints. "Psychosomatic," said the doctor. "All pastors' wives
have problems like this." I shamefacedly agreed with his
diagnosis and meekly accepted his prescription for still more
medication—this time a tranquilizer.

The pain and stiffness intensified. I tried desperately to
ignore it. Then I tried hot baths, liniments, sleeping in
certain positions. I woke up each morning in a haze of pain
and needed help getting out of bed. Once I was up, my joints
gradually loosened until the aching was tolerable. I refused to
give in to a psychosomatic illness.

One evening a friend visiting at our home asked why I was
hobbling. When I explained my condition to her, she became
very concerned and suggested that I see an internist. Perhaps
there was more to my problem than a general practitioner
could handle. It was a new thought for me. I picked a name
out of the telephone book and rang for an appointment.
The nurse asked if it was an emergency, and I quickly
reassured her that it was not. The appointment was made for
the following week. It was a long and torturous weekend.

The internist I had so blindly chosen was a kind young
man, very precise in his speech and mannerisms. He asked a
lot of questions about my background and living situation and
was especially interested in all of my psychosomatic problems. His questions became more and more specific, and his
face became very grave.

"Tentatively I would say you have rheumatoid arthritis," he
said finally. "At least let's hope so."

My head whirled. Rheumatoid arthritis! I had once met a
woman with rheumatoid arthritis. She was a friend of my
grandmother's. She was in a wheelchair, and her limbs were
so grotesquely twisted that I was embarrassed to look at her.
Grandma had told me that she was in constant severe pain. I
was young! I had a husband and two little children depending
on me.

"*Hope* it's rheumatoid arthritis?" I said faintly. "what could
be worse?"

"Have you ever heard of lupus erythematosis?"

I hadn't.

"I hope I won't have to explain it to you," he said softly. "I'll schedule you to go into the hospital tomorrow for some tests."

I went out into the waiting room and right into Tom's arms. This was a whole new dimension. A physical problem? Fear clutched at me.

That night I held onto Tom fiercely until medication finally put me to sleep. I woke up as the first light sifted into the window, and groggily made my way to the bathroom. There I fainted in a heap on the floor. Tom said I stopped breathing for several moments. He called for a friend to come for the children, bundled me into the car, and rushed off to the emergency room of the hospital. We later heard the doctor say that I had fainted from a combination of pain, anxiety, and medication.

A few days later Dr. Brinkman sat at my bedside to explain lupus to me. It had been confirmed by all the tests. I had a disease that I could neither spell nor pronounce.

Systemic lupus erythematosis (SLE or lupus for short) is a strange and elusive malady. Each person who is so diagnosed has a slightly different version of it. It is an autoimmune disease; somehow the body's mechanism for fighting off infection goes haywire and body parts are attacked instead. Frequently the kidneys become the focus of the attack; this was so in my case. It was as if both of my kidneys were transplants and my body wanted to reject them. The prevailing theory is that lupus is caused by a virus to which some of us, by heredity or for unknown other reasons, are susceptible while most people are not.

Lupus is found most frequently in women between the ages of twenty and forty. The reason for this is a mystery.

Severe damage comes to the body when a "flare" occurs, but lupus can go into remission. Remissions might last months or years. Some people never have another flare after their first. Some die from their first.

The symptoms of a flare are vagueness itself. Fatigue,

mental depression, a sore throat, stiffness, pain in the joints or muscles, a slight temperature, rashes, loss of weight—all are suspect. Others might shrug off a slight cold or a mild case of the flu; for those of us with lupus, cold or flu symptoms could be flare symptoms. Even if they are not, the cold or flu could bring on a flare. We "lupies" (my own word) become very sensitive about our health.

Flares sometimes follow a severe infection, but they can also result from any type of stress—over-fatigue, emotional difficulties, even such common things as exposure to sunlight or the smell of paints or ammonias. Sometimes there is no apparent reason for the onset of a flare.

Lupus is controlled by cortisone and some of the same medications that are used for transplant patients. These last reduce the body's ability to fight off infection. This is to keep the body from fighting itself, but it also weakens the person's ability to fight off common germs and viruses. It becomes a vicious circle. The medication is no guarantee that the flare will not occur.

My quiet and precise doctor told me only a part of this on that soft October afternoon; I absorbed even less. All I knew was that I was having a severe flare that was attacking my kidneys, and that he felt it necessary to send me to the Mayo Clinic in Rochester, Minnesota, for further tests and a kidney biopsy to assess the damage already done.

"If you can make it the first year, you have a pretty good chance. I think you can do it," he said as he left. With that remark my life with lupus began.

TWO

After the doctor left, the room seemed filled with a heavy and unnatural silence. I looked around and was surprised to see that everything looked so ordinary. Surely if the news I had just received was true, the whole world should be radically changed. But the drab green walls were the same as before; so were my crumpled white sheets.

A pile of library books still were stacked precariously on my bedside table. I flexed my fingers and toes. Heavy medication had eased the arthritis and I felt fine. There didn't *seem* to be anything wrong with my body. I glanced up and saw the smiley-face I had taped to the wall opposite my bed; it still grinned at me in the same happily vacant way.

I tried to think of the name of my disease; I couldn't get past "lupus er-." I didn't know how to spell it. I didn't understand how it went about devastating my body. It was all so alien.

Suddenly I had no intention of letting this monstrous thing intrude on my life. I would ignore it and sooner or later life would return to normal. I jumped out of bed, threw on my robe and went down to the waiting room at the end of the hall. Perhaps I would find a woman's magazine with some new recipes. I had boxes of untried recipes at home and yet I was always on the lookout for more.

A meticulously dressed woman, probably in her late forties, sat quietly in the waiting room that afternoon. She seemed much too disturbed for magazines. I was curious, and it took only a minute of polite conversation to find out that her husband was in coronary care with a massive heart attack. She was allowed to visit him for five minutes out of every hour, and time seemed an eternity as she waited for those precious five minutes. We talked for a while, but I could think of no real words of comfort. Finally I made up an excuse and left.

Next I went over to the other side of the hospital to visit an elderly man from our congregation. Only a short time before, Ted and his wife had been strong members of our church, respected for their goodness and their wisdom. Then his wife had died; he'd had a stroke; and suddenly he found himself a weak and bewildered old man. It was a hard adjustment.

When I got to his room I found Ted's family in great turmoil. A nurse had just inserted a catheter so that Ted wouldn't be constantly wet from his own urine, and he was trying his best to pull it out. It hurt, and it was definitely an insult to his already badly bruised dignity. I had worked in a nursing home as a nurse's aide and had encountered the same problem before. Gently I took Ted's face between my hands, so that he would focus on what I was saying, and explained the catheter as simply and positively as I could. After a while his body relaxed and it seemed that he was somewhat satisfied.

The family and I talked of the normal things—crops, canning, happenings at church, and then they asked the inevitable. How was I doing?

"Oh," I said nonchalantly, "I have a disease called lupus. They're sending me to Mayo's in a few days for more tests." Something tightened in my chest when I said that, but I took a deep breath and felt better.

As I left the room Ted's daughter said, loudly enough for me to overhear, "Isn't she brave?"

Brave? What did I have to be brave about? Slowly I walked back to my room.

The afternoon crept on. I tried to read. At any other time I would have savored the idea of a couple of uninterrupted hours for reading, but now my mind refused to focus on the words.

I tried to sleep, but thoughts of what was happening at home kept me from relaxing.

I talked with my roommate. She was an elderly lady who found a great deal of satisfaction in complaining about the hospital, her relatives, and life in general. We had very little in common, and the conversation lagged.

Suppertime finally came, and with it came Tom. He perched on the side of my bed and drank my tea while I ate. He talked busily of the things that were happening back in Miller. My mother had arrived to take care of the boys, and she wanted detailed instructions on what to feed them and when to nap them. Mom is a great "picker-upper"—she likes everything neat—and we laughed together at the image of her trailing after Jon and Peter constantly cleaning up everything they pulled out.

I reminded Tom that it would be Peter's sixth-month birthday in a few days. I had cupcakes in the freezer, and I wanted him and Mom to have a little celebration.

"Put him in his high chair and let him at it," I instructed. "Then take a picture so I can see too."

A silence fell and I toyed with my ham. Finally Tom said softly, "The doctor called me today. He told me what you have."

"We'll make it," I said lightly.

"I'm especially sorry about Jennifer." His voice was hesitant. Jennifer was the name we had picked out for our adopted daughter.

The room began to spin, and the food in front of me was suddenly nauseating. I pushed away the tray and said carefully, "What about Jennifer?"

Tom was dismayed. "The doctor said he told you, or I

wouldn't have mentioned it. We have to cancel our application."

No adoption? It was the one happiness I had clung to fiercely. Now Tom was saying that there would be no little girl with almond shaped eyes and glossy black pigtails. No Jenny in a long dress trailing a Raggedy Ann doll. At that moment it all came into frightening focus.

I had a disease, an *incurable* disease. It would change my life—if I indeed lived!

Nothing would ever be the same again. I looked at Tom and saw both love and fear on his face; his expression seemed to intensify the reality of the situation. Mutely I reached for his hand. We held onto each other tightly for a long time, neither of us speaking, each thinking our own painful thoughts. There was some strength just in our touching, and I hated to give it up. But Tom was so tired. At home he had two little boys and my very concerned mother waiting for him, plus the normal responsibilities of the congregation. He hadn't eaten dinner, and he had a half hour's drive home. I urged him to go, insisting I was all right.

As I watched him reluctantly go down the hall I fought back tears; the heaviness threatened my chest again. The smiley-face grinned at me mockingly. And to make matters worse, my roommate started grumbling about her food.

"Cabbage," she muttered. "Corned beef and *cabbage*. With my intestinal problems I have to watch what I eat. From the way they're taking care of me here, I'll never live long enough to see my grandchildren grown and married."

I stared at her in disbelief and despair. "I'd be happy to see my *children* grown," I cried out, and I fled blindly from the room.

People stopped and stared as I ran down the corridor. Tears streamed down my cheeks and I breathed heavily to keep from crying out.

Somehow I made my way to the hospital chapel. There,

kneeling before the tiny altar, I put my head in my hands and cried with harsh and loud sobs. My head whirled in panic. Never had I felt so frightened or alone. Death? My mind refused to comprehend it. An incurable disease? Something that would never go away, something that would twist and mold every day that I lived!

I cried selfish tears that evening. Tears for all that I had ever taken for granted, that now had been savagely ripped away by the doctor's ugly diagnosis. The secure love we shared as a family. Caring for our little boys. The dreams we had for the future. Our plans for a daughter. I had truly been walking in the sunshine and had been carelessly unaware of its gentle warmth. The doctor had said that I must avoid sunlight; was this symbolic of my future? Was I to spend the rest of my life under a cloud?

I cried other tears too—tears of anger and frustration. How could God do this to me? I was so young; I had a husband who loved me and children who needed me. What kind of stupidity would allow my life to be crippled when I had so much to offer?

Someone else was in that chapel. It was the woman from the waiting room, still waiting for her five minutes with her husband. I had noticed her when I came in, but I had ignored her in my need to be alone. She was kneeling in the last pew, her head bowed, her rosary in her hands. After a long while she came over to me and put her arm around me in a motherly way.

"Can I help?" she asked softly.

My sobs prevented a long explanation. I finally got just enough control to say, "The doctor said I could die. I have two little children at home."

She tightened her embrace and said firmly, "God loves you. He'll always take care of you. You do believe that, don't you?"

My first impulse was to laugh at the irony of the situation. Her husband was at that moment hovering between life and death. She didn't know I was a pastor's wife, supposedly a

pillar of faith. It should have been my role to comfort her.
But even as I searched for an adequate reply a strange feeling
of peace came over me and my body relaxed. The tightness
in my chest was gone.

"I believe it," I finally said, faintly.

My new friend prayed a short prayer for me and then
quietly left the room. I never saw her again. I don't know her
name or if her husband lived or died. I do know that God put
her there in that chapel at that specific time to utter those
challenging words to me: "God loves you. He'll always take
care of you. You do believe that, don't you?"

The panic and anger were gone. It was like the calm after
a violent storm. Peace, and yes, a strange feeling of joy welled
within me. I couldn't understand either feeling; both seemed
so inappropriate to my situation. But I accepted them
gratefully and without question. My peace and joy were
childlike, having no thought for the past or fears for the
future. God loved me. He was in control. The miracle had
begun. From that point he was to lead me gently into a
growing understanding of what Christian joy is all about.

THREE

The hospital chapel echoed silence as the last of the afternoon sun glimmered through the miniature stained glass windows and then faded into dusk. I felt surrounded by an almost physical sense of warmth and by my new and strange sense of peace. For a long time I knelt in the stillness, feeling but hardly daring to think.

I did make an attempt at audible prayer, but all I could think to say was *thank you*, over and over. Besides, I felt in such close communion with my God that words didn't seem necessary. He knew me, he knew all I was up against, and he was in full control of the situation. It was hard to leave that sanctuary; I didn't want to lose what was so newly found. But finally I got up and slowly made my way back to my floor.

A handsome young man was lounging in his bed across the hall from my room. We had smiled at each other on several occasions and had even waved once or twice, but he had never left his room and I hadn't wanted to intrude. Now he was listlessly watching an old rerun on television, and on impulse I stopped in to talk with him. (I wasn't being altogether altruistic; I still didn't feel like facing my roommate!)

I discovered that he was also in for tests, and we soon got into a lively discussion comparing doctors, the relative merits of hospital regulations, and our opinion of hospital food. He had a quick and droll wit, and I truly enjoyed sparring words with him. But as we talked I felt inside me a rising swell of nausea. Finally, and hastily, I excused myself. I barely made it back to my room before I started vomiting.

I threw up again and again at regular intervals far into the evening until nothing was left but dry and painful retching. Finally I fell asleep, physically exhausted but still strangely exalted. The nausea made no difference; God was in charge.

My waking thought as the nurses' aides started their fresh water ritual at six A.M. was Psalm 118:24: "This is the day that the Lord has made; let us rejoice and be glad in it." The words reverberated in my head as clearly as if someone had spoken them. For a long moment I savored the assurance of that verse, and then reality tried to rush in. *You have an incurable disease. You're in the hospital. You're still nauseated. Soon a lab worker will come for more blood.* But those realities didn't overwhelm my spirit. It was a curious feeling to think those thoughts and yet stay detached from them.

My smiley-face caught my eye. I wondered how I could have thought it was mocking me the day before; it looked so innocently joyful in the early morning light.

I chatted cheerfully with the inevitable lab worker as she drew several more vials of my blood. Then I made a stab at making myself look presentable. It was a terrible effort. Go to the bathroom. Wash my face. Comb my hair. Brush my teeth. Gratefully I climbed back into my rumpled bed and closed my eyes.

Breakfast came and went untouched. Tom stopped by briefly. He held my hand as if I was fragile. He talked but he made no mention of the pain he knew he had caused by mentioning the adoption cancellation. He told me that the doctor had contacted him and that he would be taking me up to the Mayo Clinic in Rochester the next day. Mom wanted to see me before I went. Could the boys come too?

I mostly listened and nodded, too weak to talk much. I wanted to share my feeling of peaceful joy with him, but I wasn't sure what to say. Nothing was really in focus, not yet, and anything I would say would sound like just so much brave hot air. Lupus had become a wall between us, changing our relationship and hindering the free communication I had always cherished. He kissed me gently on the forehead and left.

The morning crept by. My roommate, whom I had by now dubbed "Miss Chronic Complainer," talked on and on, but I barely heard her. The nausea had become almost a permanent part of me by now, rolling in waves as I lay as still as possible. My mind was strangely quiet.

In the afternoon Tom came with a wheelchair and took me to the reception room to see my family. Mom had tears in her eyes as she placed Peter on my lap. Jon had already found a box of well-used and mismatched toys and was earnestly at play. While Mom and Tom awkwardly made small talk I watched Jonathan and rubbed Peter's fuzzy red head with my cheek. These were my children. So beautiful. So beloved. I tried to join in the conversation, but it was an effort, and I was glad when I finally went back to my room. I wondered when I would see my boys again. But I still felt content and detached. It wasn't something for me to worry about. God was in charge.

The trip up to Rochester the next day was uneventful. Tom put the front passenger seat down so that I could almost lie down. He tucked me in as gently as we tuck the boys into bed at night. I clutched an emesis basin "just in case." For the first few miles he talked determinedly, but we soon lapsed into an awkward silence. I had really looked forward to the two-hour trip as a time alone together, but it was with relief that we finally reached St. Mary's Hospital.

The Mayo Clinic itself is for outpatients. Hospitalized patients go either to St. Mary's or to Methodist Hospital. As we waited in a small examining room for me to be admitted,

Tom noticed that someone had inadvertently left my records on the desk. It was too much of a temptation; he picked them up and began to read out loud. "Edith A. Reuss. White. Female. Age 27." So far correct. "Probable diagnosis: systemic lupus erythematosis with extensive kidney involvement." It sounded so coldly impersonal. Tom continued. "Social history: is pastor's wife; does not smoke or drink."

I looked at Tom in disbelief. "Does it really say that? Show me!" He brought over the folder so I could see, and we both suddenly began to laugh.

"Is pastor's wife; does not smoke or drink." "Tom," I sputtered, "they never even asked me if I smoke or drink. What a stereotype!" We held onto each other and laughed some more. The awkwardness between us melted; the walls came tumbling down.

"Tom," I said, suddenly serious, "I want you to understand. We can conquer this thing. We have each other and we have a loving God." Tom took my hand and nodded. Lupus was now a part of us, not just of me. Contentedly we waited together for the first of what would be a long succession of doctors.

It was a delicious feeling to be once again tucked in a cool, clean hospital bed. I had no responsibilities except to submit to a series of examinations and answer endless questions. Interns examined me. Resident doctors examined me. Finally, with almost audible fanfare, an elderly and distinguished-looking gentleman surrounded by younger doctors walked in and announced that he was my doctor.

"I'm Dr. Ward," he said with quiet confidence, "and I'll take good care of you. Now where *is* my stethescope?" An underling hurriedly handed him one. His examination was done deftly and skillfully. Several times he stopped to explain a point to the others and then they would solemnly nod and take notes. He asked only a few basic questions.

"What day is today?" he demanded of one young man.

"Tuesday, sir," was the reply.

Dr. Ward turned to me. "We'll have you out of here in a week, hopefully with the kidney biopsy completed. Do you know what a biopsy is?"

I nodded. It had already been explained to me that a small amount of my kidney tissue would be extracted by the use of a long hollow needle. He smiled at me, patted my hand, and strolled out, leaving the others to gather up his examining equipment.

"Well, Lord Ward," I thought in amusement, "if you aren't the caricature of an absent-minded professor! Hope that means you're brilliant!"

I didn't keep my supper down that night and I wasn't allowed breakfast the next day because of testing. So I became physically weaker and weaker. But at the same time I began to take an intense interest in what was going on around me. I learned the names of the nurses and something about their families.

I developed a deep sympathy for my roommate, a three-hundred-pound diabetic who had been placed on an eight-hundred-calorie diet. In spite of my nausea I still winced at the meagerness of her meal trays. She was weighed twice a day on a special industrial scale that had to be dragged in by three nurses (she weighed too much for the conventional hospital scale), and this embarrassed her deeply. Her doctors were perplexed by the fact that she didn't lose weight, and I didn't have the heart to snitch on her.

She came from a large and close-knit family, all of them hearty and heavy-set, and they visited her several times a day. To cheer her up they sneaked in cookies and other goodies which she hid in her night stand and devoured when the nurses weren't around. The whole family was used to a coarse and loud manner of talking, and it amused me no end to see how painfully they worked at cleaning up their language when they discovered that I was a pastor's wife. Often they'd slip, glance at me sheepishly, and try to correct themselves.

My childlike peace continued. I didn't think beyond each

day. Every morning I woke up with the by now very familiar verse echoing in my head: "This is the day that the Lord has made; let us rejoice and be glad in it." The words "incurable illness" lay at the back of my mind constantly, much like the presence of an aching tooth, but I avoided probing at it just as I would have avoided probing at a sore tooth with my tongue.

Only one thing broke through my calm. A soft drink commercial on television had a group of young people from all over the world singing, "I'd like to teach the world to sing in perfect harmony . . . " In the front row was a young Oriental girl, looking earnest and lovely, and somehow I identified her with the Jennifer who might have been ours. I fought back sudden tears every time that commercial came on. But the tears were always ended by the time the program came back.

Days passed. I was on a soft diet by now. And I barely touched my food. Orders were given to record both my intake and my output; no one talked openly about the specter of complete kidney failure.

Lord Ward, as I still called him, stopped in daily with his entourage of eager young men and women. They carried his professional instruments, told him the time (he was always forgetting to wind his watch), and eagerly hung on his every word. It wasn't until months later that I discovered that my nickname for him was unusually apt. Lord Ward was chairman of Mayo Clinic's board of governors and he accepted very few patients. I had indeed been most fortunate.

One afternoon Tom came in full of excitement (he was making the two-hundred-mile round trip daily). The congregation had of their own accord decided to have a prayer service for me. Without consulting him they had planned it, notified the whole community, and finally, almost as an afterthought, invited him. It was to be that night.

"How sweet of them!" I exclaimed. "But it really isn't necessary. I'm not *that* sick!"

"They want to do this for you," he said simply. I was a

little embarrassed; I was spiritually so high and had so little concern for my physical well-being, and they were putting in such an effort.

That evening I ate my supper and managed to keep it down. Later, feeling a little stronger, I asked the nurse if I could take a shower. (I was in an older part of the hospital and our bathrooms contained only a stool and a sink.) She offered to get me a wheelchair and take me. And so it was quite by coincidence, if you want to believe in such a thing, that at the very time that our congregation was gathered in prayer for me I was taking my first shower in days, with hymns of joy bubbling from my lips while I lathered up.

It felt so good to be really clean. It was a very basic, natural feeling, and for the first time I became a little homesick. I didn't want to be a sickie anymore. When I couldn't get to sleep that night I grabbed a book and wandered down the hall (no wheelchair!) to a small reception room.

The room didn't look at all hospital-like. The sofa and chairs were shabby and plump, not sleek and plastic, and in one corner was a large glassed-in cabinet housing the largest collection of Hummel figurines that I'd ever seen. What a curious place for such a collection! I dearly love Hummels, and I spent a long time admiring each one before I curled up with my book. The curtains had been left open, and the soft lighting in the room allowed me to see out without glare. I alternately read and gazed out at the starlit sky, finally relaxed in body as well as in spirit.

I was truly hungry for breakfast the next morning, but I got none because of more testing. Tom came at the same time as my lunch tray, and I groaned to him about my aversion to broth, Jello, and tea.

"You're hungry?" he asked in disbelief. "What *do* you want?"

I didn't hesitate; I'd been dreaming about it all morning.

"A bologna sandwich with lettuce and mayonnaise," I said promptly.

Tom stared at me, grinned and disappeared. Fifteen minutes later he was back with my sandwich. (I never did learn where he got it.) Never before or since has anything tasted so good! I ate half and put the other half away to savor when Tom was gone.

Tom was full of news of the prayer service—who had come, who led the praying, what songs were sung. It had touched him deeply. Neither of us put into words what seemed so obvious; the prayer service had "worked." The absence of nausea and my renewed strength were indeed parts of a miracle. But that sounded so presumptuous at the time that we were unable to talk about it.

The next day I was unexpectedly allowed to go home. My blood platelet count was still too low for the kidney biopsy. (Platelets help the blood to clot.) I needed rest and medication, and could get those at home. The biopsy would be scheduled as soon as the platelet count was up. My release was an unexpected treat for me and for Tom. He whistled happily as he helped me get my things together. I had lost weight and we giggled together about how baggy my clothes looked. Mostly we looked forward to surprising Mom and the boys.

On the way home we stopped at the church so Tom could take home some unfinished work. The president of the congregation was there picking up his mail; he was a large, no-nonsense German with a crewcut, and he had always slightly intimidated me. Now he threw his arms around me.

"The prayer service worked," I told him. "Thank you for having it." When he released me from his bear-like hug I noticed a single tear glistening on his cheek. I was deeply touched.

Mom was thrilled to see me and soon was bustling around fixing soup and sandwiches for Tom and me. The boys climbed all over me. The kitchen was warm and bright and beautifully familiar. I was home!

PS 118:24

FOUR

When I woke in the morning I felt like shouting out what
had become my theme verse: "This is the day that the
Lord has made . . . !" For on that day that verse glowed
with a richer and deeper meaning. I still felt the security
that God was in charge, but he had now allowed me a new
dimension to my feeling of inner peace and joy. I was
home.

The sheets were soft to the touch, so unlike hospital
bedding. Tom breathed evenly in his sleep, close and warm.
There would be no tests, no blood taking, no probing, no
questions.

Our neighbors had invited us over for one of their famous
company breakfasts, and my mouth watered at the thought of
the mounds of food to come—eggs and bacon and sausage
and pancakes, all washed down with juice and milk and
plenty of good coffee. Even the sky seemed bluer outside my
window as I cuddled in next to Tom and luxuriated in my
plans for the day. After breakfast there would be time for a
long talk with my mother, and then I would read to Jon and
play with Peter. If I felt strong enough I could even help a
little with the meals. The world seemed to contain more
happiness than I could bear.

The days passed swiftly and happily. My platelet count went up and the biopsy was scheduled for early the next week. On Sunday I went to church and was amazed at the richness of our Lutheran liturgy. "We praise thee, we bless thee, we worship thee, we give thanks to thee for thy great glory . . . " (*The Service Book and Hymnal of the Lutheran Church in America*, page 20). Never before had those words been so meaningful; I literally bounced in time to the music as I sang.

Being the preacher's wife has its small advantages. During the time for announcements I went to the lectern to thank the congregation personally for their loving support of the past few weeks. The casseroles and cookies and offers to care for the boys. Their generous admonition to Tom to take off as much time as he felt he needed to be with me. I needed to thank them especially for the prayer service, and to tell them how my weakness and nausea had subsided that same night. I told them about my upcoming biopsy and asked for their continued prayer support. "But I want you to know," I ended up, "that there is nothing to be worried about. I thank God and I thank you."

Ted, the elderly man I had visited in the hospital, died unexpectedly, and his funeral was scheduled for the same time as my biopsy. At first this upset Tom, but since I was planning only a three-day stay at the hospital, it seemed silly to plan the funeral around me. I persuaded him to take me up to Rochester, settle me in, and come to get me two days later.

I was on the same floor as before, and I felt a comradeship as I greeted the nursing staff. My roommate this time was a seventeen-year-old girl battling leukemia. Kate was in for transfusions and was trying desperately to be nonchalant about the whole thing. When I asked how the other kids in her school had reacted to her illness, she shook her head vigorously.

"They don't know," she told me. "I told them I need

transfusions because I'm anemic. I don't want them to look at me like I'm some sort of freak!"

Kate paid a lot of attention to her hair and make-up. And she chattered incessantly and knowledgeably about the handsomest of the young interns. But late that night, after the lights were dimmed and the nurses were tiptoeing instead of stomping down the hall, her nonchalance evaporated.

"Edee," she said after a long silence, "are you afraid of dying?"

I thought about my biopsy the next day. There was certainly an element of risk there. I thought about the disease eating away at my body.

"No," I finally said, "I guess I'm not. I figure that God has given me so much happiness here on earth as a small taste of what it will be like in the next life."

"Do you really believe in a heaven with angels and harps and that kind of thing?"

"No," I told her, smiling at the thought of me strumming a harp. "I don't have any theological foundation for it, but I suppose it's sort of like when you wake up in the morning, all cozy and warm and happy, before you've had time to let problems crowd into your mind. I imagine it's just a perpetual feeling of joy."

"That sounds more realistic," she said flatly. "I can believe in that kind of heaven." With that she rolled over and went to sleep.

I lay awake for a long time, really considering for the first time the possibility of dying. For the past few weeks I had been relaxed and unconcerned about the future. They tell me now that I came close to death during those early days in the hospital, but I had not thought about it then. Was I afraid? No, I had told Kate the truth. For me dying would be only a transition to a state that held even more happiness for me.

And I had no real regrets. I had a good relationship with my parents. I had gone away to a college that I dearly loved.

My world had expanded considerably during my college years, and I had experienced the thrill of satisfaction of earning my degree with honors. I had been chosen in love to be the wife of a man I could deeply respect, and I had learned to love him back with the same openness that he demonstrated. Out of our love we had conceived two healthy boys, and because I had used natural childbirth the second time around, I actually had felt the indescribable sweetness of Peter's body slipping out of mine. I knew the deep contentment of nursing a child and the thrill of having someone trustingly call me "Mommy." I had friends and family who loved me openly and unselfishly. I had so much!

I looked over at Kate's sleeping form and felt a pang of guilt. Most likely she would never experience the things in life that had meant the most to me. I thanked God that night for all the beauty he had already crowded into my life, and then I too slept.

The next morning I was wheeled through what seemed like miles of corridors to the X-ray department for kidney X-rays. It was a most uncomfortable hour of lying still on a cold hard slab while dye was pumped through me and a huge overhead machine took picture after picture. As I waited for a nurse to take me back after it was all over I had a chance to observe the other patients coming and going. It wasn't a pretty sight. Grotesque deformities and severe accident cases made lupus seem like a rather tame thing to have. Again the greatness of my blessings was brought home to me.

In the early afternoon a nurse came in to offer me a tranquilizer.

"What for?" I asked.

"Oh, most people want them before biopsies. The doctor will deaden the immediate area so that you can be awake to breathe at the proper times. That can be pretty nerve-wracking." She gave me a long look. "Don't take it if you don't think you need it," she finally said.

"I don't need it," I replied, smiling.

The biopsy itself was almost fun. The doctors, plus a kidney specialist and the inevitable residents and interns, assembled in a small operating room and talked gravely and quietly. They checked my X-rays which were hung all over the walls, and they marked up my back with some sort of black magic marker. In the meantime I carried on a heated discussion with the nurse about the hospital practice of putting the husband's name on women's identification bands.

"I'm proud to be Tom's wife," I told her, "but I'm a separate person, especially here. He's not being biopsied; I am. You'd be much more comforting if you called me by my first name instead of Mrs. Reuss. Besides, no one ever even pronounces it right."

"Is your husband here?" asked one doctor (probably to divert me!).

"No," I told him with a quick grin. "He's a preacher and he has a funeral right now. Isn't that morbid?"

"She refused the tranquilizer," I heard someone say in a low voice.

"I'd say she has a built-in tranquilizer," said someone else.

I grinned again, this time to myself. A built-in tranquilizer! He didn't realize what a funny and yet apt definition he had just given of faith in a caring God!

I breathed in all the right places (giving credit to my natural childbirth classes), and soon was back in my room. It was necessary to lie flat on my back for twenty-four hours to minimize the risk of internal bleeding, a physically uncomfortable time, but the nurses had to take my blood pressure at regular intervals, and sometimes we got so involved in our conversation that they would realize with a start that it was time for another pressure check. I talked awhile with Kate, knit awhile, watched television awhile, and dozed most of the night.

Tom came the next afternoon, and we waited for hours at the Mayo Clinic to see Lord Ward, who wanted to tell me the biopsy results and give me instructions regarding my medication. When we finally were ushered into his office he looked very grave.

"The damage to your kidneys is extensive," he said gently, "and kidneys don't repair themselves. That means that you'll always have more pain and less strength than other people."

"Can I take care of my family?" I asked bluntly.

He considered. "As you get stronger—and right now you're considerably weakened by your flare and hospitalization—you'll be able to handle light housework and look after your children. Just remember always to rest when you get tired. Don't try vacuuming or carrying heavy loads of wash. Remember all the things I told you to avoid, like the sun and the smell of paint. And stay away from people who have colds or the flu."

Then he went on to caution me about my medications. I was already on a high dosage of cortisone, and cortisone produces many side effects. My face would round out until it looked like a chipmunk carrying nuts in its cheek. My hair would thin out. My appetite would increase but at the same time I would put on weight more easily. I would tend to retain fluids, so I had to watch my salt intake. Cortisone tenses muscles, so I might have trouble with insomnia. Stomach ulcers could occur. So could depression. In the long haul cortisone causes a weakness in joints and muscles; it even causes cataracts.

It was a long list and he didn't spare me. But as he talked I hugged to myself the promise that soon I would be caring for my family again. The flare was over! This time I was going home for good!

Home! Home was Tom's happy grin. Home was Jon prattling on about Halloween and Peter tentatively starting to creep. Home was being put in the capable hands of Mom Reuss, who had come to take my mother's place. Home was a deluge of telephone calls and letters and visits from people reminding me of their love and concern. Home was more food brought in than we could possibly use. Homemade breads and brownies and stews and casseroles, much of which went into the freezer for the days ahead when I wouldn't have the energy to prepare them myself.

I was almost embarrassed by the great show of love that was poured upon me. For one thing, I certainly didn't deserve it. For another, how could I possibly repay all of those people?

I talked about this to Mom Reuss one morning as we drank tea together. Tom's mom is a very wise woman.

"In the first place," she told me, "love is never deserved. It just is. You don't get love by being good enough or acquiring enough points with the person who loves you. And you don't repay them for what they do for you. You accept their gifts graciously and then somehow pass it on to fill any other needs you see that *you* can meet. You probably won't be able to make meals or babysit or do the other things that people are doing for you, but you'll find your own way."

We talked about love for a long time that morning; the ideas we discussed were mind-expanding for me. Love is not earned; it has to be given freely. And once you receive it, you cannot hoard it or it will die. Love lives only if it is received openly and passed on freely. Each person, given his own set of talents and abilities, remolds the love he is given and then must pass it on. What a beautiful way to live!

Time passed. Tom and the boys carved pumpkins and I roasted the seeds. We took Jon and Peter trick-or-treating in the car so that I could go along to witness their excitement. Tom's mom left after a week, confident that with the help of our congregation we would manage. At first I was apprehensive, but gradually I was able to take over small duties around the house. I dusted. I planned menus and cooked simple meals. I changed Peter's diapers. I entertained Jon. Each new thing was a triumph. My first trip to the grocery store was high adventure, even though it made me so tired that I had to wait in the car while Tom checked out. The first time I cleaned the toilet bowl I felt a thrill of satisfaction at doing something so completely ordinary. I was a homemaker again!

There were limitations. Tom and others did what I couldn't manage. The ladies continued to occasionally bring in food. When I had a bad day someone was always available to take over the boys so I could get more rest.

We fell into a routine. Tom worked his schedule so that he was home for an hour after lunch each day so I could rest. Then Jon would go to his room for a "quiet hour" while Peter took his nap. During this time I had the opportunity for reading and meditation. It was a time to sort out my ideas and expand my mind.

Thanksgiving came. The vastness of my blessings was again emphasized. Christmas came with its own measure of happiness. The usually dreary months of winter seemed light. Tom commented often on how changed I was. Before, I had worked so hard at being the Perfect Wife, the Perfect Mother, the Perfect Homemaker, the Perfect Pastor's Wife. I had expected the impossible of myself and had wound up exhausted and disgruntled with the whole world. Now I couldn't possibly do everything. I just didn't have the physical strength, and there was always the threat of another flare if I overdid. I was forced to straighten out my priorities.

I couldn't clean the bathrooms and still take the boys for a walk. I often chose the walk and was almost surprised that the house didn't collapse because of my dirty bathrooms. I couldn't bake bread and still make beds. Because I love to bake, we ate homemade bread happily while the beds stayed unmade. At night I couldn't watch television and still have time to spend with Tom, so the TV went off and we spent long hours sitting by candlelight, sharing ideas and daydreaming.

It sounds unrealistic now to say that during my first year of being a "lupie" I was always content, always grateful. And yet it was pretty much true. Well, the soft drink commercial with its lovely Oriental girl still had the power to tighten my

chest and bring tears to my eyes. And occasionally I was
frustrated by my inability to fill a need I saw in the
congregation. I was hurt the day the ladies cleaned the church
and refused to let me come help. I felt a tug of resentment
when others planned an afternoon swim, forgetting that I
couldn't join them because of my need to stay out of the sun.
But these were all petty and fleeting feelings. I did not
question *why*.

It seemed obvious at the time that lupus had brought me a
greater measure of human joy than I had ever before
experienced. I was occasionally in pain and I suffered some
insomnia, but these seemed like a small price to pay for my
general happiness. It was all very black and white, all very
child-like. It was a time of complete and unquestioned
reliance on what had become a very personal God. It was a
time of strengthening for the growth that was to follow.

Faith is not static; if it is, it dies. It must grow. And I soon
learned the truth of the old adage that growth comes through
pain.

FIVE

Every three months I had an appointment with Lord Ward
at the Mayo Clinic. I saw my Mason City doctor frequently in
between. Always I heard the same thing—the lupus was still
in remission and I could cut back a little more on the
cortisone. The threat of another flare receded from our
minds; lupus seemed a thing of the past. Only my extreme
fatigue and occasional annoying problems with the cortisone
remained.

Although Lord Ward seemed always to forget the obvious,
he had a wonderful capacity for remembering things about
his patients that couldn't possibly be listed in the medical
records. On one visit he asked, "You were going to adopt,
weren't you?" I nodded, not knowing what he was getting at.
"I won't make any firm promises," he said, "but if you
continue as well as you're doing now, we'll talk about
adoption again." The picture of my almond-eyed, pigtailed
Jennifer popped into my mind. She was still possible!

Summer came, and except for my routine afternoon rest I
did pretty much as I had the year before. I canned and froze
and made jam. I "spring housecleaned." using lots of hot
soapy water instead of ammonia type cleaners. We took the
boys for picnics and swims, mostly in the evening because the
low angle of the evening sun makes the rays harmless. But

after a while I even became careless about that. I couldn't see any bad effect from exposure, and I felt that big hats and sun-screening creams were an unnecessary nuisance.

For our vacation in July we boldly decided on a trip to Canada for a reunion with two couples who were friends from seminary days. Bill and Leone lived in North Dakota and would meet us in Winnipeg where Dennis and Carol had a parish. From Winnipeg we would all go to a lake cabin owned by one of the members of Dennis' congregation. At the last minute we decided to take along my teenage brother Bruce; it was a trip we knew he'd enjoy, and we welcomed his help with the driving and the children.

We arrived in Winnipeg in a flurry of tears and bear hugs and joyful squeals. Although it had been only a year since we had last been together, it seemed like an eternity. During our years at the sem we had, along with a fourth couple who were in Ethiopia, become as one family. We had shared each others' homes and meals. We had cried and rejoiced and supported each other in such close-knit fellowship that it had been a searing experience to graduate and go in separate directions. We had promised to get together after a year.

After the initial rush of emotion, however, we all sort of retreated and began to look each other over. Once we had been as one, but the year apart had been event-filled for all of us. The men had been ordained and were now pastors. Carol and Dennis had had their first child. Leone and Bill were expecting their second. I had discovered my lupus. Had we changed much? More important, had our relationship changed? We talked far into the night, interrupting and crowding each other in our attempt to make ourselves known again.

The next day we drove up to the cabin and discovered that it was small but had its own lovely and isolated beach. We women divided up the sleeping space—three-year-old Jonathan was the oldest of four boys—while the men unloaded Dennis' boat and found canvas and poles to make me a shelter from the sun on the water's edge. In high spirits they pronounced me their queen and settled me in on a reclining chair. Then they all changed into their swimming suits and plunged in.

For the next few days I had a ringside seat to watch the adults cavorting like children in the water and the children building sandcastles with the sober concentration of adults. Peter was still none too steady on his feet, and I laughed until tears came when he stalked out into the waves with Tom at his side and lost his balance—time after time after time. He just didn't seem to learn. The days were light and frivolous; we seemed a long way from the pressures and social demands of the ministry.

Only at night did things become awkward. The mosquitoes drove us into the cabin early, and after we had bedded down the children, we tried to have the same depth of discussion that we enjoyed in our seminary days. Somehow, after we all had described our churches and parsonages, and had finished "shop talk" about our individual church activities, we fell into silence. Somehow we couldn't get down to the feeling level.

Once I tried to describe how lupus had brought me to a new level of contentment, but I couldn't get the words right. It sounded terribly goody-goody even to me. We all tried hard, but we never really jelled into the unit we had been. For me it was a valuable lesson in change. I still loved them all, but we had gone on to different lives.

When we got back to Iowa I was exhausted and achey. I went to the doctor, who concluded that I was very close to having a flare. "Not enough rest and too much sun" was his verdict when I described my vacation. Somehow I had forgotten that the sun's rays are reflected off water and sand. So even though I had stayed in my shelter, I had terribly exposed myself. Dr. Brinkman upped my cortisone to the level at which I had started almost a year before. And he advised more rest.

A week later Tom was scheduled to be a resident pastor at

Riverside Bible Camp in Story City, Iowa. The boys and I
were invited along. My only responsibilities were to act as
advisor to some of the small group Bible studies and mingle
with the campers as I wished. I would have no housework to
do or meals to fix. It seemed like a golden opportunity to get
the rest I needed.

The morning we were to leave, I woke up with a great
deal of pain in my knees. I called the doctor and he upped
the cortisone half again as much as I was already taking. I
was up to ninety milligrams daily.

"You're definitely having a flare and that's the highest
dosage I can give you," he said. "There's nothing else we can
do." He noted that my next regular Mayo visit was scheduled
for a week from that Monday. I would have to wait until
then. I told him about camp, and he agreed that it was a
good place for me to be. "Just rest!" was his final order.

Camp held a happy promise in spite of my painful knees.
At the opening session for counselors I explained my
problem and asked for their prayers. The compassion on
their fresh young faces encouraged me and cheered me. This
would be a fun week! I had never gone to Bible camp as a
child, so the prospect of campfires, weenie roasts and
canteens seemed a dream come true even with the reality of a
flare nagging at the back of my mind.

Quickly the dream became a nightmare. The pastors' cabin
was new and still in the process of being painted. The smell
of fresh paint gave me a severe headache, and I was
concerned about its effects on my lupus. The weather turned
drizzly-cool, and the chilly dampness of my sleeping bag
added much to my discomfort. The pain in my knees
increased drastically.

It got to the point where I couldn't walk from my cabin to
the mess hall or to the campers' cabins where the Bible
studies were held. Ever-resourceful Tom went in search of a
wagon to carry me, and came back with a wheelbarrow.

Jonathan and Peter begged for rides, so Tom dumped them in with me and we took off with Tom making loud engine noises. We laughed, but tears were very close to the surface.

Finally the pain got to be too much. I felt so walled off by it that I couldn't communicate well with others, much less concentrate on Bible studies. Tom was carting me around and caring for the boys; I felt guilty because he was neglecting his camp duties. I suggested that he take me and the boys to stay with a friend in Waterloo for the remainder of the camp week. Lynn and I had been college roommates. She had been maid of honor at my wedding and was Jonathan's godmother. I knew that Lynn and her husband Gary would willingly take care of us. Reluctantly Tom agreed, but he decided to keep Jon with him. Jon was loving camp and was an unusually independent little boy; Tom was sure they could manage. We called Lynn and made arrangements for the following morning.

That night I stayed in my bunk instead of going to the campfire, and the wife of one of the other pastors came in to see me. Agnes Lee was warm, motherly, and very concerned about me. She had heard that I was leaving. She wanted time to pray with me before I left. She also brought a book that she wanted me to read—*Power in Praise* by Merlin Carothers. Agnes was extremely enthusiastic about the book. I wondered how it would apply to my situation. I would soon learn the book's premise—that we should thank and praise God for all that happens in our life, no matter how evil it seems. God does not allow anything to happen to his beloved children that can't be turned to use for their good and his glory.

"Try thanking him for your lupus," she said gently. "I don't know why he gave it to you, but I believe you will somehow benefit." We prayed together and she left.

I was left thoughtful. Praise God for my lupus? And yet, wasn't that exactly what I had been doing the last months? It

seemed obvious that lupus had turned my life around, had
made me more appreciative of my blessings, and had altered
my priorities. But I was having *another* flare. According to
my doctor I was at that very minute most likely having more
kidney damage. And I would be left even weaker than
before—if they managed to control the flare at all. My knees
throbbed relentlessly. The heavy dosage of cortisone made me
bloated and tense. I was inconveniencing everyone around
me. "What's the benefit of that?" I thought miserably.

Tom came back from the campfire with the boys—a
hyped-up medley of sticky ice-creamed faces, smoky clothes,
and damp tennies. It took a long time to settle them down,
but finally Tom managed it. I told him about the concept of
praising God for everything and asked his opinion. He
thought seriously before answering.

"I don't want you to suffer," he finally said. "Right now I
can't thank God honestly for your pain. But I trust him and I
know that he loves you."

We clung to each other a long time, voicing our mutual
fears and taking comfort in just touching. Then we prayed,
"Thy will be done." It was all we could do.

Lynn welcomed Peter and me as if taking care of us was
the most delightful thing she could think of. She quickly
settled me into a warm, dry bed with a heating pad and a cup
of mint tea. She spoiled Peter quite unashamedly. At that
time she and Gary were still childless, and all of her maternal
instincts fell on lucky Pete. She sang to him, fed him animal
crackers, and rocked him to sleep. Peter adored her.

My pain subsided somewhat under Lynn's care; we spent
long hours talking, and the time passed pleasantly.

On Thursday evening Tom called to check on me. He was
still praying, he said, and the camp staff was praying. And
one more thing—on Friday night the staff, including the
pastors that week, would be having a special healing service
for me. They were going to use Tom in my place, utilizing

the laying on of hands and anointing with oil. They were
going to ask for complete healing. Would Lynn and I pray in
accord?

Lynn and I thrashed it out all day Friday. It would have
been simplest just to go along with Tom's request, but there
seemed to be so many unanswered questions involved.

First of all, if I was to praise God for the lupus, how could
I at the same time pray for it to go away? It was like
attempting to drive in two directions at the same time.

Then there was the nagging thought that perhaps I really
didn't want complete healing. It had limited my activity. If I
were whole, would I be able to maintain my new priorities,
or would I go off again on the Perfect Wife, Perfect Mother,
Perfect Pastor's Wife kick? Lupus was my crutch. Besides—
and here I was being brutally honest with Lynn and myself—
I had at times enjoyed my image as the brave but cheerful
invalid. It got me out of a lot of unpleasant work and made
people notice me. Could I honestly pray for complete
healing?

I saw yet another stumbling block. A serious one. I was
afraid to pray for something so specific because I didn't know
what would happen to my faith in Christ if I wasn't healed.
The laying on of hands and anointing with oil seemed almost
to be hocus pocus, a form of manipulation. What kind of God
responded merely because we used the right formula? If we
went through with the ritual and prayed for complete
healing, if I let myself believe whole-heartedly that the
healing would be done, what if it weren't? I would have
reached out and found nothing. I would have to say that
either God wasn't listening or there was no God at all. The
very basis of my life would be shattered. Perhaps it would be
better not to make this "test," better to leave well enough
alone.

I shared all of this with Lynn. Unlike my own quicksilver
faith (up one minute and down the next), hers was always

strong and steady. She wanted to pray for healing—she didn't like the idea of my being in pain—but she wanted to temper her prayer with "thy will be done."

"God knows our needs better than we do," she reasoned. "How can we *demand* anything of him?"

Deep within me I agreed, but Bible passages on prayer kept leaping into my mind:

"But, dearly loved friends, if our consciences are clear, we can come to the Lord with perfect assurance and trust, and get whatever we ask for because we are obeying him and doing the things that please him" (I John 3:21, 22).

"And so it is with prayer—keep on asking and you will keep on getting; keep on looking and you will keep on finding; knock and the door will be opened" (Luke 11:9).

"You can get anything—*anything* you ask for in prayer—if you believe" (Matthew 21:22).

Could we not take God at his own Word? I was confused and ambivalent.

The appointed time came. Lynn pulled a chair up to my couch and we held hands. Each of us prayed silently. I don't know what Lynn asked for, but I mostly offered up as honestly as I could my mixed bag of emotions and questions. I ended up with "Lord, I have to thank you for how you've used my lupus, but I also know you can heal me. I don't need further kidney damage. Heal me if it is your will. Amen."

We waited for a while in silence. I didn't feel any different. The pain in my knees was still there. I still was achey tired. Finally we began to talk of other things.

When Tom came to get me I had a lot of questions about the prayer service and his feelings about it.

"Didn't it give you a hocus pocus sensation?" I asked.

"No," he answered carefully. "God so often works through ordinary means—bread and wine, the water of baptism. Who am I to say that he doesn't work through oil and the laying on of hands?"

"I still hurt," I reminded him.

"Wait and see," was his response.

Usually we considered our Mayo visits mini-vacations. We left the boys somewhere, went up to Rochester the night before my appointment, and found a reasonably nice motel. When we got away early enough we went out for supper. Otherwise we brought along pop, potato chips, and chip dip, and made a little party in our room. The next morning I'd go for my lab work and to see Dr. Ward for a short examination. We were then free for the rest of the morning and noon hour to shop and have lunch at some place close to the clinic. Wong's Restaurant became our favorite. After lunch we would go back to the clinic to see Lord Ward for the lab results. We usually got home again by supper time.

This trip lacked the light-heartedness of our previous Mayo visits. I kept wondering if healing could be done on the inside when I still felt so miserable outside. The lab tests and examinations would tell. I wondered if healing sometimes happens gradually. I wondered if I believed "enough" to have a prayer for healing answered. If only it had been instantaneous—whappo-zammo—everything gone! If only I could have left Lynn's like the lame man in Acts 3, "walking and leaping and praising God"! Then it would have seemed proof positive of a loving and personal God. But I had left Lynn's hobbling.

The next morning I dutifully took care of the lab work and then went up to see Dr. Ward. His examination was thorough.

"I think we have a bad flare here," he said, shaking his head. "I can't give you any more cortisone. If the lab report is what I expect, the only thing you can do is to resign yourself to complete bed rest for a couple of months."

Bed rest! With two little boys? I was so proud of my growing self-sufficiency. I got my afternoon appointment and went tearfully to the waiting room to tell Tom the news.

I *was* having a flare. Prayer had not stopped it. Who knew what was ahead? We held hands tightly and left the clinic.

Lunch should have been the high point of the day, but we didn't feel like experimenting with fun foods. We ended up having a meat loaf plate luncheon at a nearby drugstore; somehow that offered more of the comfort of the homey and familiar.

We talked nonstop. How would we manage if I was bedridden? Would we have to send the boys to my parents in Milwaukee? Tom certainly couldn't manage alone, and we couldn't lay such a heavy burden on our congregation. We went back to the clinic with aching hearts.

Tom accompanied me into the consulting room; bad news would be better heard together. We had run out of words; we just held hands and waited.

Dr. Ward looked puzzled when he walked in. He was reading my lab report with sober concentration.

"I don't understand this," he said. "You're having no further kidney damage. All the tests are similar to the ones you have been having the past year. I think we should talk about cutting back the medication."

There had been no instantaneous healing; the lupus was still there, but *there had been no further kidney damage.*

On the two-hour trip home we sang songs. The one we sang over and over was a simple round we had learned at camp. It came from Philippians 4:4—"Rejoice in the Lord always; again I say rejoice."

Matt 21:22
Luke 11:9
Acts 3
Phil 4:4
1 John 3:21,22

Ps 118:24

SIX

In the next few weeks the pain slowly subsided. With a lower dosage of cortisone I began to feel more like my old self—at least on the outside. My experience with the prayer service should have convinced me once and for all of God's activity in my life; there was just no other explanation for the lack of kidney damage. Yet I had looked honestly at my faith in those days between the healing service and my Mayo visit, and I could not deny what I had found. It was the opening of a Pandora's box.

Even though faith had never come easy for me, my whole life had been based on the premise that God was Reality, specifically in the person of Jesus Christ. My moral system was based on that premise. My relationship to others, even my marriage, was based on it. I was the wife of a Christian pastor. What would happen if I became brutally honest, if I announced that I was an agnostic, that I wanted Christ to be real but I just wasn't sure? What would that do to those around me? On what would I base my life? No, I *needed* Christ to be real whether I felt his presence just now or not. I would have to live, if not in faith, at least in the hope of faith.

Then there was the problem of joy. I had rejoiced at the

doctor's report but hadn't been able to keep the "high." At
night when I couldn't sleep, or while I was going about
routine chores, I thought a lot about joy. I could not deny the
reality or intensity of the joy I experienced in the hospital.
Where had it gone? I remembered the grateful joy of the
past months. Even that was gone. Before, I had daily counted
my blessings; now my mind nagged at me—realistically, I
seemed to have a lot less to be thankful for than most
people. The lupus was there to stay; who knew when I'd
have another flare and this time have kidney failure? I
wondered if this latest flare had put my dreams of adopting
in jeopardy. Rejoice in the Lord always? I could put on a
good act, but the term "hypocrite" scathed me.

And yet—good had come out of this flare. My weakness
had again made me dependent on Tom and on the members
of our congregation, and I was reminded anew of their love
and concern. Maybe even this agony of self-examination
would result in a renewed faith.

Someone new came into my life soon after that. Ro Short
had been a member of our church all along, but I knew little
more than her name. She and her husband Bill were faithful
in worship. You couldn't miss them as they came trooping
into church with their seven boys, always noisily and a shade
late. But they took no part in the social life of the
congregation—and we had no time for anything else. I knew
that they had made an application for a daughter through
Holt, the same agency we had applied to; and knowing this
made it all the harder for me to get to know Ro. I was
jealous.

One day Bill and Ro called and asked if they could stop in.
"Sure," I said, though I couldn't imagine what they wanted. In
they came, bearing gifts of fresh eggs and garden produce.
We fussed over coffee and thoroughly discussed the weather
and the prospects of a good harvest. Finally they relaxed and
came to the point of their visit.

"Our application for Holt has been approved," said Bill

nervously. "Now we're waiting for them to pick out a little girl for us." We made the appropriate happy noises.

Bill continued. "We know you had planned to adopt a Korean, so we know you have no prejudice against Orientals. Would you consider being her godparents?"

I could see Tom was speechless. For a change, I was too.

"Maybe you can't because you're our pastor," Bill added hastily. "That's OK; we won't be offended if you say no."

Tom glanced at me and smiled. "We'd be proud to," he said simply.

"Good!" exploded Ro with her natural exuberance. "We'll share her!"

Ro and I visited together often after that. At first we talked mainly of what was happening in the maze of paperwork that the Shorts needed to wade through, but gradually we began really to know each other.

Ro (short for Rosemarie) knew Christ and was almost carelessly confident in his love for her. Because of that love she was free to be exactly who she was deep down inside. She almost always wore pigtails and overalls, the most practical attire for the farm work she so dearly loved. She saw housework as unnecessary window dressing; time was much better spent reading to a child, canning windfall apples, or delivering baby pigs. Their old farmhouse was always in shambles, but no one cared. Noisy love was the keynote in the Short household, and Ro was its center.

Ro always welcomed me with squeals of delight; she was never too busy for a visit. She'd take Jon and Peter out to do something fascinating with her own boys (like gathering eggs or jumping in the hay), and then we'd settle back with our tea and talk for hours. She was widely read. She had strong opinions on almost everything; she was impatient with bureaucracy and wanted injustices corrected *right now*.

"Doggone it!" she'd explode when we talked of school segregation or the Viet Nam war or any topic dealing with hurting people, "why don't the authorities do something!"

We talked often of faith. I shared my struggles with her and found her a sympathetic listener. She encouraged my questions. She considered my relentless probing honest, and thought I would come out of it with a much more mature faith.

Cynthia Marie came from Korea after months and months of the kind of bureaucratic red tape that Ro so hated. Cindy was a tiny girl, just a year old, with sparse dry hair and unhealthy-looking skin. She alternately whimpered and screamed in Korean the night the Shorts brought her home from the Minneapolis airport, and she refused to be comforted by anyone but Bill. Ro and I decided that she was perfect.

After only a few days in her new home Cindy began to relax and eat everything in sight. Her skin took on a healthy glow, and her cheeks began to fill out with a hint of real baby fat. Ro and I admitted to each other that our only disappointment was that until she was of school age Cindy never had enough hair for the pigtails that we had dreamed about.

Suddenly summer had come again. Tom loves the mountains, so we decided to use our vacation and continuing education time to go to the Academy of the Rockies—a place I privately labeled a "Bible camp for pastors." For two weeks each year the Academy takes over a resort in the heart of the Rocky Mountains. Pastors and their families have the option of staying at the lodge or in individualized cabins or at a nearby campground. Lecture series for adults and organized recreation for children take up the morning; the afternoons are free and some type of group activity is planned for most of the evenings.

It was a great vacation. We stayed in a cabin and had our own chipmunk to feed. We popped corn in our fireplace and explored nearby Estes Park. We marveled at the majesty of the mountains all around us.

At first I wasn't particularly excited about the prospect of morning lectures, but I had brought along my knitting and figured the time wouldn't be completely wasted.

The main speaker was Richard Jensen, assistant professor of systematic theology at Tom's alma mater, Wartburg Seminary. His topic was "The Theology of the Cross." That sounded tedious and too academic for me. I sat back to knit one, purl two. In just a few sentences, however, Jensen had me sitting on the edge of my chair, my knitting forgotten in my lap.

"Christianity does not equal human happiness," he said. "Look in the Gospels. Our Lord wasn't always happy. He cried unhappy tears over Jerusalem and at the death of Lazarus. He suffered great anguish of soul in the Garden of Gethsemane. He didn't accept the cross light-heartedly! It's when you deliberately reach out to God in the darkness, when you aren't happily 'feeling' his presence, that you experience the deepest faith."

It was as if a cloud had shifted and rays of understanding were lighting up every corner of my soul. I didn't have to be "happy" over the problems of my life. That wasn't the meaning of true "rejoicing" at all! I could be free to admit the anger and frustration and hurt that I felt. I could even admit to God that I didn't always feel that he was real. I was free . . .

Jensen also uttered a warning for Christians. "Don't expect that as a Christian your life will be untroubled, or that you'll be able always to handle trouble graciously. It's easy to dwell only on the glories of Easter. But you have to remember that there was first a Good Friday. You must pause at the foot of the cross on your way to the empty tomb, for without the cross the tomb is meaningless. There are no shortcuts."

Dr. Jensen's lectures would have been plenty to make the Academy worthwhile, but we had another lecturer who confronted me in an entirely different areas.

Dr. Lee Griffin, a Christian psychiatrist, talked to us about the unique problems that plague a pastor and his family. He especially zeroed in on the loneliness and hurt often expressed by pastors' wives. They're pushed into activities of the church regardless of their own needs and abilities. They're made to feel guilty when they resent the church's intrusion on their time with their husbands. They sometimes get so wrapped up in their husbands' calling that they neglect their own.

"Don't seek all your gratification in the church," Lee told us. "Find another outlet. Search yourself prayerfully. Discover some talent or ability that is truly your own and then develop it! If you don't, you're not giving full credit to the Lord who created you and your talents. If you don't, you're cheating yourself and your marriage because you're not everything you could be."

Lee fired me up. I wanted to run right out and do something wildly creative, something not at all connected with Faith Lutheran Church in Miller, Iowa. But I immediately dashed my own sky-high dreams. What could I do? I did have social work training, but a job outside the home was unthinkable. With my kidney damage and need for rest I had all I could physically handle with housework and our two boys. There seemed no extra time or energy to "develop my potential."

Late one night Tom and I sat in front of a crackling fire in our cabin, talking quietly so we wouldn't disturb the boys sleeping in the next room. I admitted my feeling of defeat in the face of Lee's challenge.

"I'll just have to wait until the boys are in school," I said dejectedly. Jon was four. Peter was two. School seemed a long way off.

Tom persisted. "Daydream a little," he urged. "Was there ever something you really wanted to be?"

I thought a long time. Crazy things ran through my mind. Ballerina. Movie star. Foreign diplomat. But then I remembered my sixth-grade teacher. Miss Pavcek was the strictly no-nonsense type; she was not given to compliments. Just before I graduated to junior high she took me aside and said, "You have a talent for writing, Edith. Someday I will expect to read your first book." I had dabbled in journalism in high school, but writing seemed so frivolous. I put it aside when I entered the more academic world of college.

"A writer?" I said to Tom, waiting for a snort of amusement. It sounded so presumptuous!

Tom didn't bat an eye. "Great!" he exploded. "You wouldn't have to be away from home or strain yourself physically."

I had immediate and obvious objections. Who said I could write? I could hardly act on the opinion of a long-ago sixth-grade teacher. Besides, who could concentrate on writing with two little boys always at hand? By evening when they were both in bed I was too tired.

Tom thought some more. He can become very stubborn.

"How about a baby-sitter one day a week?" he asked. "It wouldn't give you much time, but it's better than none."

I protested. We didn't have the money, and who would we get anyway?

"Ro," said Tom simply.

I felt a glimmer of excitement. Maybe it was possible. Jon and Peter adored Ro and her happy-go-lucky bunch. If Tom was willing to gamble baby-sitting money on my completely undeveloped "talent," maybe I should be willing to try it too.

Years later I asked Tom what had given him confidence in my writing ability when he had never known me to write anything more literary than a letter to my mother.

"Sanctified dumbness," he answered with a grin. I think he was right.

When we got home from our vacation I immediately called Ro and told her our idea. She was delighted. She'd love to have the boys, and it excited her to know she was helping to develop a "famous author." Her enthusiasm was contagious. I hadn't yet written a word, but already I was a Writer! Ro refused the money we offered her, but I finally persuaded her to put it in a special account for "our" Cindy.

I learned to cherish my "professional days," as Tom termed them. ("If I call it your 'working day' it sounds like you don't do anything the rest of the week," he explained.) By nine in the morning the boys were gone and the house was reasonably straightened. I had my personal devotions and then sat down importantly with pen and scratch pad. I knew nothing about manuscript form, and my style was undeveloped, but I doggedly wrote on. I wrote short devotional articles and children's stories and sent them off with high hopes. One by one they came back to me; I collected a large pile of rejection slips.

Months went by. I became discouraged, but I so enjoyed my "professional days" that I didn't want to give up. Besides, Tom and Ro had such confidence in me that I was ashamed to give up. And then one day we went to pick up our mail and I found in it a check for fifteen dollars. I had sold my first article! I went home and called Ro, and then I whooped and hollered and jumped all over the furniture. To celebrate, we blew the entire check at a pizza place. I was no longer just Edee Reuss, wife, mother, homemaker. I was also Edith A. Reuss, Published Author.

SEVEN.

For the most part I continued to be content. The lupus stayed in reasonable remission. The boys grew and became more independent; Jon started kindergarten. I sold just enough articles to keep me encouraged about my writing. Tom's ministry seemed to blossom. Whenever I needed to really talk, I had Ro to turn to.

Tom and I came to an awareness that while we seemed to be growing closer and closer, we were still very distinct individuals. We sometimes experienced the same things differently. We had different opinions on some social issues. We knew that most of our goals were in common, but one night we sat up late with candlelight and soft music to discuss our individual dreams for the future.

"What one thing do you want most?" I asked him. It didn't take him long to answer. He'd had the same dream since before I knew him.

"I want to go to Israel," he said, "not on a ten-day tour but for an in-depth stay, perhaps working on an archeological dig."

"What do you want?" he asked me.

It took me a long time to answer.

"I'd like to publish a book," I finally said. It sounded audacious coming from someone who had sold only a handful of articles.

"Fine," he said. "Now how can we make our dreams come true?"

I laughed. "I'll write a book and send you to Israel with the money," I told him. It sounded a little silly, but somehow it also seemed just a little possible. After that evening we started to put away small sums of money for his trip and I made my first abortive attempts at a book describing my ups and downs with lupus.

I worked at my "book" sporadically, but I spent a lot of time thinking and writing about my faith. It wasn't easy. I knew that I gave the image of the ever-cheerful, steadfast Christian, and it would have been nice to just accept that image as reality. But I was still struggling. Again and again Jensen's "You have to stop at the foot of the cross on the way to the empty tomb" passed through my mind. On my good days I embraced that thought wholeheartedly; on my bad days I resented the fact that my cross seemed so much heavier than others'.

The long trips back and forth to Mason City to see the doctor began to burden us. I wasn't yet strong enough to drive myself that distance, and the trips cut deeply into Tom's free time. Grocery shopping was difficult. We had always known that Jonathan was bright, but now we were discovering that he was considered exceptionally gifted, and we worried about his schooling. It occurred to us that living in the country was a luxury that we really couldn't afford. We went to Des Moines and discussed all of this with a member of the Iowa District staff. Almost reluctantly we put Tom's name in for a new call.

The idea of moving was two-edged. It was exciting to think of a new ministry in a city; it was devastating to think of leaving Miller and the feeling of closeness we enjoyed with so many people there. Besides, the people of Miller understood my physical problems and had been more than generous when Tom needed time to be with me and the boys. Would we find another congregation so accepting?

We had several "feelers" but none panned out. Tom said that we would have to wait for "God's timing," but I'm so terribly impatient. When God says wait, I get frustrated.

Then one day while I was resting I received a call from Stan Carlsen, pastor of Central Lutheran Church in Des Moines. "We're looking for an associate pastor," he said. "Tell me about your husband."

Des Moines! One of Tom's deepest interests was church-state relationships. Living in Des Moines where he'd have access to the state legislature seemed too good to be true.

I wasn't sure how to answer Stan. "He's a great preacher," I said hesitantly. "He's good at counseling and he's interested in politics."

Stan asked if we could come down for an interview the following week. "Sure," I said. I didn't even know Tom's schedule.

I caught a cold and couldn't go with Tom to the interview. He came back elated.

"The church is only a block from the State Capitol!" he said with awe. "I'd have a chance to work with the legislature! And another thing—one of the call committee members has a sister-in-law with lupus. She immediately understood and sympathized with my need for a more flexible schedule."

Central Lutheran in Des Moines sounded too good to be true. I wondered how much we dared to hope. . . .

We had another call from the call committee. Could they come up to Miller to hear Tom preach? They offered to scatter themselves in the congregation so that no one would suspect that they were a committee interested in snatching away their pastor. I laughed. Faith Lutheran in Miller was so small; how could six strangers be inconspicuous?

The committee came. I spent so much time in the service keeping Jon and Peter especially quiet (and watching the committee members for their reactions) that I failed to worship. Afterwards I couldn't even remember the theme of Tom's sermon.

After the service we invited the committee to lunch. I had prepared the food ahead of time, the boys were especially well behaved, and the committee members seemed approving of us all. They didn't commit themselves, however, and after they left we settled down to the agony of waiting.

A few weeks later we were really discouraged. Surely if they were interested in Tom he would have been notified. Maybe Des Moines wasn't for us. Maybe we'd have to wait for another call. I got very impatient with the Lord—and with the call committee of Central Lutheran in Des Moines.

Lynn and Gary came from Waterloo to be with us for a weekend in early December. We went to a Christmas concert at Waldorf College in Forest City, and there met Gene Hermeier, a pastor from Des Moines whom we knew slightly. Gene's daughter Kristi was a student at Waldorf.

"Congratulations on your call!" Gene boomed.

Tom and I looked at each other hesitantly. "I was only interviewed; I don't have a call," Tom told him.

Gene looked thoroughly puzzled. "But the congregation met last week and voted you in. I read it in their newsletter."

Tom had the call! We hugged joyfully and then Lynn and I danced right there amid all of the concert goers. Our letter of call didn't come for several more days; it had been misdirected at the post office.

After that the days flew by. Amid preparations for Christmas we took time to go down to Des Moines to buy a home. Central would give us a housing allowance rather than a parsonage. We began the awful chore of packing. The heaviest job of all was trying to explain to the people who had done everything possible to make us feel one of them. How could we love them and still want to go?

I most dreaded telling my next door neighbor, Inez. Inez had a heart condition and she lived alone. She had often been reassured by the fact that we were always available to get her car started or to shovel her out. She knew that I watched for her shade to go up each morning, her signal to me that she was well. I knew I had to tell Inez about our decision before someone else did.

When I tried to explain, my explanations fell flat. We sat together in silence for a long time; hurt was written all over her face.

"I wish you weren't going. I'll miss you," she finally said. Inez possessed both a simple piety and a blunt openness. She had often steered me through sticky social problems and had been a voice of common sense when I wallowed in too much self-pity. I knew I would miss her too.

All of the good-byes were hard. I cried through the church Christmas program. I left a little piece of myself with each family who invited us over for a meal "one last time." The night before we actually left, we took our dog Tramp over to the Short farm. Tramp was a big outdoor country dog. Moving him to the city would have been cruel. Ro and Bill rejoiced and cried with us. They gave us ten dozen eggs and a half bushel of soybeans to take to the city. We promised to write lots of letters.

Des Moines was a startling contrast to Miller. We were delighted by the convenience of doctors and shopping, but we felt stifled by the closeness of the houses in our neighborhood. It was especially oppressive because we didn't even *know* the people who surrounded us. Tom's sister lived in Des Moines. For the first time we would have "relations" around. But I felt a little empty not knowing even the names that went with the faces in the next pew at church. We had learned to understand Miller's social pattern and the way the congregation operated. Now we were intimidated by Central's size and formality. We loved having our own home, but it was a no-nonsense type of house, and I missed the little quirks that had made the Miller parsonage so appealing.

We settled in little by little. A few neighbors stopped in, and we discovered that we had unknowingly picked a home on a block populated by a preponderance of little boys Jon's and Peter's ages. We enrolled Jon in a special school where he could be a part of individualized reading and math programs. Soon even Peter finally stopped asking when we'd go home.

I naturally had a new doctor. Dr. Smith appeared much more optimistic about my prognosis than my cautious Dr. Brinkman in Mason City. He seemed so very optimistic that on my second visit I asked about the possibilities of adopting.

"Why not?" he shrugged. "Just don't ask for a tiny baby or a child that would require constant attention."

Jennifer! The next morning I sat down and wrote to Holt. We were really going to get her this time!

After a few weeks we got a reply—a letter asking us all sorts of questions indicating that we had perhaps not thought this out carefully. Would I be able to cope with another child? If I became seriously ill, how would we manage? Would the child suffer because of my lupus? I wrote back page after page assuring them of the normality of our home and our loving desire for a daughter. We enclosed a report from my doctor stating that it was his medical opinion that I was capable of handling a third child. Then we started waiting for their decision. It was similar to waiting for the call letter, but I was even more impatient. I had already waited four years!

A letter from Holt finally arrived. A short letter, much to the point. They were denying our application because of my disease. I stormed and cried and tore the letter into little pieces. Then I sat back and thought some more.

We had one more possibility. Iowa Social Services. Our daughter wouldn't be the Korean child we had been envisioning through the years, but we would still have a daughter. We put in our application, stating that we would take any hard-to-place child except one that would require heavy physical work for me. We went to marathon group sessions; we filled out form after form; we had home interviews. Everything seemed right. I began to overflow with happy love for the little girl who would soon be ours.

Our caseworker was young and gentle. "Why do you want

a daughter?" she asked me once. How can you explain a dream in rational terms? Whatever I could say sounded silly. I wanted a daughter so I could braid her hair. I wanted a daughter so I could buy her long dresses and a Raggedy Ann doll. I didn't care if the dresses stayed in her closet and the doll was stuffed under her bed. I just wanted to buy them. I wanted a daughter so someday we could bake cookies together and I could tell her the sweetness of being a woman.

When I confessed those things to our caseworker she didn't laugh. She told us that she was approving our application and would put us on a waiting list.

In the meantime Dr. Smith was so pleased with my health that he decided to cut out my cortisone completely. First, however, he wanted a kidney biopsy to see exactly how things stood. He had a friend who was also a kidney specialist. Would I consent to a biopsy?

"Fine," I said. "Anything to get off the cortisone."

I went into the hospital in high spirits. Almost I felt guilty about inconveniencing my family and piling up hospital bills while I had what I considered a mini-vacation. The kidney specialist, Dr. Catherine Condon, was also the head of the teaching department in Methodist Hospital in Des Moines. She asked if I was willing to be put on the teaching floor and to subject myself to a flock of interns and residents. Naturally I agreed; all of the attention just added to the fun.

Dr. Condon was demanding of herself and her staff, but she was warm and intuitive toward her patients. I was especially impressed with her question, "Would you like me to explain everything to you or would you be more comfortable not knowing?" It was a good and basic question, but I had never been asked it before. I did want to have everything explained in careful detail; I was more easily frightened by the unknown than by any identifiable problem.

The biopsy was a little uncomfortable, but it went well and I was home the next day with only the time-worn demand to rest. I expected a glowing report.

Two weeks later Dr. Condon's secretary called. By some
fluke all of the tissue that had been extracted was scar tissue;
there would have to be another biopsy.

A month later I went in again, and at first this
hospitalization seemed a carbon copy of the first. I had the
same nurses and doctors; even the menus were the same. In
the biopsy room I was asked the routine question, "Are you
allergic to iodine?" I pooh-poohed the idea.

"I had this done last month—no problem," I said.

They injected the iodine (used to trace the position of the
kidney) and almost immediately my lips began to swell and
my neck began to itch. I was allergic to iodine. For a minute I
was afraid they'd have to cancel the biopsy, but they gave me
an intravenous antidote, and the symptoms disappeared.

When one nurse started to take the intravenous tube out of
my arm another stopped her. "Leave it in," she suggested.
"It's in a good position just in case we need it."

The biopsy progressed smoothly. I held my breath
whenever they needed me to, and I watched a small TV-type
screen as Dr. Condon gently positioned the hollow needle
into my body. It occurred to me that my head was starting to
feel light and I was a little nauseated.

"Don't be ridiculous," I scolded myself. "How can you be
squeamish this time around?"

But the room began to whirl. I turned my head away from
the screen and closed my eyes. From far away I heard voices,
"She's stopped talking . . . check her blood pressure . . . she's
in shock!"

"I'm dying," I thought dreamily. "So this is what it's like to
die. How curious that I'm neither scared nor sad."

I felt the table tilt so that my head was down. I heard feet
scurrying. I was hooked up intravenously. "Thank goodness
we left the tube in her!" someone said.

After what seemed like eons my head cleared and I
cautiously opened my eyes. I smiled weakly at the faces
bending over me. I wasn't dying after all.

Although my blood pressure remained dangerously low for the rest of the day and into the night, I was allowed to go home on schedule. I was awfully weak, though, and it took several weeks to get back my old strength. Over and over Tom and I marveled at what could have been a close brush with death. What if I hadn't reacted to the iodine? What if the nurse had pulled out the intravenous tube? It seemed another sign that the Lord was at work in my life.

A few weeks later I went to Dr. Smith to get the biopsy results. It wasn't at all what I had anticipated.

"You have a very insidious kind of lupus—something I didn't suspect," said the doctor. "It's a kind that never really goes into remission; damage is being done continuously. There's no medical reason why you lived past the first year. Eventually your kidneys will give out, and you're an unlikely candidate for a transplant. Dialysis is your only hope." He was nervous and started to walk out. Handing out bad news made him uncomfortable.

"Wait," I said. "What's my prognosis?"

He shrugged. "A couple, maybe five years."

"And our adoption?" I asked.

"Do what you want. I've already given my consent and I won't take it back." This time he walked out for good.

We had lived with the specter of death for years, but always it had seemed far off. A time limit like this was a different matter. In the following weeks I probed my feelings to see where I hurt.

I wasn't afraid. I wouldn't be afraid when I lay on my deathbed; my experience with the biopsy had shown me that. I wasn't angry with God. With the type of lupus that I apparently had, God had already given me time beyond what I could expect. I was sad. I had begun to hope that I would live to see Jonathan and Peter grow into men; now it seemed impossible. I would miss the people and things of this world, and I knew that I would be missed.

And then there was the adoption. We were still waiting

for an official acceptance. If we did nothing, that acceptance would eventually come. I could still have my daughter. But we had asked for a hard-to-place child. Surely she would be already scarred in some way before we got her. I thought of Cindy Short and how terrified she had been when she arrived in America. She had blossomed under Ro and Bill's tender love for her. Tom and I could do that for our own little girl . . . and then I would die. She would be hurt again. Could I knowingly expose a child to that kind of hurt? Could I be that selfish?

I told Tom my feelings hesitantly, half hoping that he'd say, "Don't be silly. Of course we'll adopt." Instead he took me into his arms and said sadly, "I've been thinking the same thing, but I wanted you to decide."

I buried my head in Tom's shoulder. "Will you call social services and tell them?" I asked. Then I cried long and hard. It's never easy to say good-bye to a dream.

EIGHT

One afternoon I sat in our rocking chair, a blanket wrapped around me and my Bible in my lap. It was close to Christmas, and I had Handel's *Messiah* playing softly in the background. I was sifting through my thoughts and emotions, doing what I laughingly call "taking my spiritual temperature."

My life was precarious. I was back to living one day at a time and being grateful for that. There would be no daughter. It was peculiar that after the first rush of bitter anguish I had felt almost a sense of relief. We had dreamed that dream so long and we had discovered that it was flatly impossible. Knowing that there would be no "perhaps someday" made me able to lay it aside and turn to other things. Our family was complete, and the strong bond that had always been a part of us tightened. I felt a fierce and possessive love for my three "men."

Peace and joy welled within me as I sat there that December afternoon. Unable to contain it, I got up and danced gaily around the room. This was the same joy I had experienced those long-ago days in the hospital, and it was just as alien to my situation.

The joy persisted through Christmas. With every carol, every lit candle, I thought, "This might be for the last time." But I wasn't saddened. I received many gifts that year, but the one I most remember was that sense of unexplained joy.

As always, time passed. Spring came and then summer. I wrote out my own memorial service and arranged with the University Hospitals at Iowa City to take my body for research after I died. With that behind me I felt free to go about my regular routines. I baked and canned and occasionally taught in Peter's preschool. And I kept writing. Writing helped me to articulate what I was feeling inside.

In August Tom asked me if I'd be willing to go to Cursillo. Cursillo is a lay movement that originated in the Catholic church and has spread to the Lutherans, the Methodists, and other denominations. On separate weekends men and women are given a real glimpse into the grace of God through a rigid schedule of talks, liturgical services, and discussion periods. Each part of the weekend builds on another; every detail is designed to remind the participant of God's love. Tom wanted badly to go but couldn't unless I went too. Cursillo demands participation of both husband and wife. I hesitated. From the little I had heard it sounded like just another churchy gimmick designed to play on my emotions. But Tom asks so little of me. I finally consented.

I went to Cursillo a skeptical martyr, but the genuine love of the people who prepared the weekend caught me off guard and won me over. I marveled at the depth of concern coming from people I didn't even know; I basked in that concern.

On the last morning I woke up early, and on impulse dressed and went to the chapel. "I'm tired of fighting you," I prayed. "Help me to truly believe."

A warmth filled me. "I love you," was his reply. "Remember that I always love you." It left a vivid impression.

One night in September the arch in my foot began to ache. Tom rubbed it and it seemed to feel better. The next morning I swung out of bed and screamed when my feet hit the floor. It was another flare.

"Complete bed rest for a week," was the doctor's order.

I was in high spirits that first week. I surrounded myself

with books and writing paper and the telephone. I made wry jokes about doing anything to get breakfast in bed. The word of my flare got out and the casseroles and cookies started coming in. But I didn't get better. The one week stretched to two and then three. I seemed to be marking time.

In the meantime Tom was scheduled to go the American Lutheran Church national convention in Washington, D.C. He talked about getting someone to take his place, but I couldn't see that.

"Don't be silly," I told him. "I'll probably be better in a couple of days, and besides, the boys pretty much take care of themselves. They can help me with the cooking and the wash, and we'll let the rest slide. I'll get lots of rest!"

Tom gave in. With Jonathan gone all day and Peter in afternoon kindergarten, I did have plenty of time to myself. Tom contacted the president of the ladies' organization of our church before he left, and she made a schedule of volunteers who would come in each day to visit. The boys and I dubbed the idea the "angel of the day program." We looked forward to their visits. We never knew who would come or what they had planned for us. Some brought meals or treats; some offered to dust or vacuum. Others knew intuitively when I just needed to talk.

We got along well for almost a week with the help of our "angels" and then I became even more tired and achey than I had been. Jon and Peter had tired of the adventure of caring for me as well as themselves; it was time for reinforcements. I called my ever-generous mother, explained our problem, and met her at the airport the next morning. That afternoon the doctor put me in the hospital.

I remember sinking luxuriously into my pillow after the first flurry of nurses and interns. I closed my eyes and could almost feel responsibility lifting from my shoulders. I didn't have to act brave or cheerful or make any decisions. I didn't even want to see anyone; I just wanted to lie there and let my mind drift.

Tom came home a few days later, and it was obvious that he felt guilty about my hospitalization. I didn't know how to comfort him, and I was too tired to even try.

I left the hospital after ten days with orders to "keep resting." The flare was over. There had been no further kidney damage. But I tired more easily than before, and the everyday arthritic-type joint pain was higher than it had been before. I rebelled futilely at the idea of living the rest of my life with that much pain.

"I love you," God had told me at Cursillo. Now I couldn't recapture the feeling.

At the end of October we received a telephone call late on a Saturday night. It was my friend Lynn. She called to tell us that her only brother Glenn had been killed in a boating accident. Lynn's voice was calm and yet childishly bewildered.

"I thought you'd want to know," she said. "Please pray for my folks and Glenn's wife."

I lay awake much of the night, heavy with the sadness of Glenn's death. I hadn't known him well, so I wasn't personally touched, but people I loved were grieving. I prayed for God to support them in a gentle way.

The next morning after church we got another call. A young mother from our Miller congregation had unknowingly backed the car over her seventeen-month-old son. Timmy lived only a few minutes. Tom and I had been especially close to Sue and her family. She had been our most faithful babysitter, and Tom had confirmed her. Now she wanted Tom to share in the funeral. First Glenn and now little Timmy! My heart ached even worse than my joints.

The air was heavy and damp the morning we drove up to Miller for Timmy's funeral. As we left Des Moines both of us wished out loud that the day was over. We would be confronted by a lot of pain and hurt in the next few hours. I knew Tom had the strength, but I wondered if I did. At least I would have some respite—Tom had insisted that I stay with Ro for a few hours so I could get my rest. That would give him time to help with the last minute funeral arrangements.

When we got to the Short farm Ro ran out to meet me and caught me in a big bear hug. Her face mirrored my own emotions—happiness at being together again and horror at Timmy's death. She shooed Tom off, took me in and settled me down with a cup of tea. Then we started to talk. We had both written voluminous letters, but there was still so much to catch up on. She told me about her new son, a five-year-old Korean boy who had arrived only a few months previously. She told me about the Laotian family she and Bill had sponsored, who were starting to be independent. She asked about Jon and Peter and my writing. After a while she forced me into a bed for my "rest," but I bounced out after only half an hour. We still had too much to talk about!

Ro shrugged off my doctor's prognosis. "You can't die," she said. "You're needed too much."

We talked about death and our aversion to funerals. I told her about donating my body for research and writing my own memorial service.

"Hey!" she said. "That's what I want, too. None of this funeral rigmarole."

"Do it, Ro," I urged her. "You have to sign papers to make it legal."

"I think I will," she replied.

I watched as Ro tried to find a cover for the gelatin salad she was donating for the funeral "lunch." It was a salad typical of Ro—molded in a big mixing bowl instead of the fancy cut glass dishes that the other ladies of the Miller church used.

"I love you, Ro," I said on impulse. "I'm so glad we got to be friends."

"I love you too," Ro answered with a quick grin.

Later, I was glad we'd had that moment. There were many people for me to talk to at the funeral itself and at the lunch afterwards. We didn't get a chance to say good-bye.

The funeral itself seemed unreal play-acting. The closed
white casket, pathetically small, looked more like an
overgrown jewelry case than anything else, and the familiar
lines of the funeral liturgy seemed to have no connection
with a boy just going on two. After the interment I went up
to Sue and hugged her.

"Please try to remember that God loves you," I whispered.
Her face was blank with pain, but her eyes answered back,
"Oh, yeah?"

I wanted so badly to take some of the burden of her hurt
on myself, but I knew that it was something she'd have to
work out herself. It seemed an unfair burden for one so
young. Wearily, we drove back to Des Moines.

I prayed for Sue and my friend Lynn that night. I wished
that I could do more than just pray. I slept very little.

The next day I was exhausted. After lunch I took a mild
sleeping pill and went to bed. I had three hours before the
boys would be home from school.

Almost immediately the telephone rang, and I felt a quick
annoyance with myself for not having kept the receiver off
the hook. It was a long-distance call—one of the young
farmers from Miller.

"Is Pastor Tom there?" he asked.

"No," I said, greatly puzzled. "Can I take a message?"

There was a pause, and then he said hesitantly, "I guess I
can tell you, but I'd rather Pastor Tom was there. Ro is
dead."

I closed my eyes. Surely my tiredness or the medication
was playing tricks on me.

"There was a tractor accident," he went on. "I was driving
by when the ambulance came, so I stopped in to see what I
could do. She was already dead. Bill wanted me to tell you.
He'll call later to talk to you about the funeral."

I think I thanked him for calling. I'm not sure. "Ro! Ro!
Ro!" was pounding through my brain. After I hung up it
turned to "No! no! no!" I whispered it and then started to

scream it out loud. I shouted and beat my fists helplessly into the bed. No! Ro couldn't be dead! I loved her! I had just seen her!

"Tom has to know," I thought, and I tried to dial the telephone. I couldn't remember the church number. I gave up and ran to a neighbor's.

Joy was a good friend. She is a Christian, and we had often prayed together. I didn't stop to knock. I ran into her house yelling, "She's dead, Joy. My friend is dead." Joy ran down from the upstairs and caught me in an embrace.

"My friend is dead," I repeated, and collapsed in her arms.

"God can't be that unfair!" I said that over and over. Joy did not ask for further explanation. I had awakened her toddler with my screaming, and he cried in an upstairs bedroom. Joy just held me close, her eyes closed in prayer. I didn't want anything to do with prayer. I cried and cried until I was spent.

Joy sat me on the sofa and called Tom. He came immediately and we cried together. Then he took me home.

The first storm was over for me; I felt an aching dullness but my rage was gone. Tom and I talked about how we would tell Jon and Peter. We remembered out loud the happy times we had shared with the Shorts. We had so much evidence of Ro's love all around us—Cindy's picture on the wall, books we had shared, the ten dozen eggs she had thrust on me just the day before. In my mind's eye I could see her bouncing happily out to greet me, her pigtails sticking straight out. It didn't seem possible that someone so *alive* could be dead. And yet she was.

Bill called that night and asked Tom to conduct the funeral. "We were like family," he said.

"I can't," said Tom. "She was too much a part of me. But we're coming up tomorrow to do what we can."

A second trip to Miller in a week. It seemed like a badly written soap opera.

It hurt to pull into the Short farmyard and not have Ro

run out to meet me. Without her, the place seemed lifeless. Her children were bewildered and wandered around aimlessly. Bill had gone to the funeral home to pick out a casket.

"A casket!" I thought, and the idea knifed through me. How Ro would have hated it. But she hadn't had time to fill out a donor application card, so her body would have to be buried. There would have to be a funeral instead of the simple memorial service that she would have preferred.

Bill came home, and Tom and I ran to meet him in the yard. We were caught in a three-way embrace. Words weren't necessary.

Lynn Helmke, the "new" pastor's wife, was there helping with the children and directing the flow of food that was already coming in—Miller's way of saying, "We care." I decided to stay and help her.

"You don't have the strength," Tom protested. "You're just over a flare!"

"God put me here; he'll have to take care of me," I replied dully.

That was Wednesday. Tom went back to Des Moines and would return with the boys for the funeral on Friday.

Lynn and I worked hard. We served meals and did dishes and tried to put together clothes for the children to wear to the funeral. Lynn had loved Ro too, and the strain on her was great. She had been the one to explain their mother's death to the youngest Short children.

At one point when Lynn was looking for foil to wrap some food she burst out, "I get so mad at Ro! She was so unorganized. How could she do this to us?"

On Thursday afternoon I went with Lynn to the parsonage to rest, but neither of us could relax. We talked together about Ro and how Bill would manage without her. How we wanted that family to stay together!

Lynn's husband, Ken, called us from the church. He was tired and discouraged. Two days before, he had struggled putting together little Timmy's funeral. Now he had Ro's, and he couldn't get a handle on what to say in the sermon. He wanted help.

I got my Bible out of my suitcase and leafed through the Epistles. I wanted something that would testify to the strength of Ro's faith and still deal with the reality of our pain. The words of 2 Corinthians 6:10 leaped out at me. "Our hearts ache, but at the same time we have the joy of the Lord."

It was a paradoxical verse. Pain and joy at the same time? It made sense to me. I had had the infinite joy of knowing and loving Ro; her death did not change that. Touching her life had been such a precious gift that it was worth all the hurt I was experiencing. I talked that over with Lynn, and she shared it with Ken. Ken used that verse as the basis for his message.

Bill was in a daze, and Ro's mother seemed to be in shock. Lynn and I found ourselves in charge of the younger Short children at the funeral. They had not been to the funeral home—Bill didn't want it and we knew Ro would have abhorred it. So when we arrived at the church we took the four youngest to the narthex to see the closed casket while the rest of the family went downstairs to get ready for a short prayer service that would precede the funeral. Daniel was ten; Cindy, just four. Six-year-old Chris had always been exceptionally close to his mother. Joey had been in the United States less than a year and still didn't communicate well in English. He seemed most baffled by the whole thing.

The four of them ran their fingers gently and reverently along the smooth grain of the wooden casket.

"Is Mom in there?" asked Dan abruptly.

"Just her body," said Lynn. She looked to me for support.

"Remember catching monarch butterflies?" I asked in a sudden inspiration. "They lived in a cocoon for a long time but in order to become beautiful and free, the butterfly has to leave the cocoon behind. Your mom is like the butterfly, free and beautiful with Jesus. Only her cocoon is in that box."

Lynn and I sat with the children through the service. From the moment I had learned of Ro's death I had been like two people—one coolly and critically watching the other rant and cry and grieve. Now I watched myself holding Joey and Dan close, whispering answers to their continuous questions:

"Is there a light in that box so Mom can see?"

"Does she know we're here?"

"Will she come back?"

"What does her cocoon look like?"

At graveside I held onto my composure by taking careful note of small details like the brilliance of the afternoon sun and the sharpness of the wind. Steve, second oldest of the nine children, was home from West Point in full uniform, and I saw him stiffen and salute as his mother's casket was carried from the hearse. I heard Ken's familiar "Ashes to ashes, dust to dust," and then I broke entirely. I clung to Tom and cried out with a pain that held all of my insides in a vise, a vise that gripped tighter and tighter.

A God of love? How could a God of love allow such a stupid thing to happen? Ro had nine children; she was so very much loved and needed. I couldn't think that God had caused Ro's death, but he *had allowed* it. He had the power to intervene and had not. Why?

My body and my mind were fatigued. The flare had so worn me down that I had nothing left with which to deal with the three totally senseless deaths. Glenn. Timmy. Ro. I really didn't care if God was real or not.

For weeks I lived in an impenetrable darkness. I functioned on the outside; I took care of the house, made the meals, talked and even laughed with others at church. But I kept God out of my soul, and my soul was empty.

I read carefully through the Psalms. I identified with and underlined every cry of pain and despair.

"All who seek for God will live in joy," says Psalm 69:32. I

had sought God and I was living in pain. I was tired of trying
to understand either God or his joy. I didn't pray. The God
who had permitted my lupus and then had allowed me to
live on in fatigue and pain while Glenn, Timmy, and Ro died
wasn't worth praying to.

2 COR 6:10

PS 69:32

NINE

God patiently allowed me my time in the darkness; he did
not intrude on my grief. But the time came when I was tired
of hurting, when I looked back with helpless longing at my
times of happy intimacy with my Lord. I remembered the
Christmas before—how I had danced around the room for
sheer joy. I wondered how I could have danced so soon after
the unexpected biopsy report. I remembered God's "I love
you" at Cursillo and wondered if I had allowed my emotions
to play tricks on me. I remembered the light-filled freedom I
had experienced when Jensen explained the theology of the
Cross. Now the darkness was so thick that it didn't seem
possible that any light even existed. I reached out to tear
away the darkness, but I was much too feeble, much too sore
from all my hurting, to do so. Finally I admitted defeat. I
couldn't reach God. If he truly loved me, he would have to
break through to me.

On one of my frequent check-ups, Dr. Smith told me
casually that recent lupus research indicated that my "type" of
lupus was perhaps not inevitably fatal after all.

"People have had the same lab results as you and then
have gone into long, unexplained remissions," he explained.
"Sometimes there never is any further organ damage. You
could very well have this kind."

A reprieve? I might live to see my boys grow up after all! There had been so many ups and downs with my disease that I couldn't work up any real elation, but for a moment there was a crack in my darkness and I caught a glimpse, just a glimpse, of the sunshine on the other side.

My friend Inez died. I went back to Miller fearfully, but although we experienced a sense of deep loss, there was no feeling of inconsolable grief at her funeral. Inez had lived a long and full life, and she had been well prepared for her death. In fact, she had at times been impatient for it. Now she was "home," and there was a rightness about it. As we tenderly committed her body to the ground, the crack in my darkness widened.

In the spring Koinonia, the young adults group of our church, had a retreat and asked me to lead a section on prayer. The outer me did so willingly; the inner me balked. Who was I to teach others to pray? But God spoke through me, and even I listened when I talked about unanswered prayer:

"We think we know what's best for our lives and the lives of those we love, but we are like little children making requests of their parents. We lack the depth of knowledge, the wisdom of knowing what we really need and what is harmful."

I shared with them how when we lived in Miller, Jonathan had thrown tantrums because we would not allow him to ride his bicycle on the blacktop. He was physically capable of doing so and thought he could be helpful by riding down to the feedstore to pick up our mail and occasional groceries. From his point of view it was very reasonable. But as parents we knew how cars barreled through the town without regard to the speed limit. We knew how immature Jon still was. If he became frightened, he was likely to steer into a car rather than away from it. We could have given in to his demands, but we showed a greater love for Jon by denying his request and allowing him to get angry with us.

Was it possible that my own pain and anger could be likened to Jon's tantrum? Would I someday understand God's lack of intervention in Ro's death as Jon would understand our refusal to let him ride on the blacktop? A tiny glimmer of light broke through.

One weekend I worked at a Cursillo—the first time I had done so. The warmth of the Cursillo team soothed and uplifted me.

In the prayer chapel someone had hung a giant banner that said simply, "All I ask of you is that you always remember that I love you." The words seared through me. Is that all he asks? Did that mean that I didn't have to somehow respond properly to that love? Could I just cuddle into it as a baby cuddles into his mother's lap? The darkness cracked some more.

Since our moving to Des Moines, Tom had become friends with Gene Hermeier, the pastor who had first told us about our call to Des Moines. We had reacted with sadness when we found out that his daughter Kristi also had lupus. She was young—still in college—and I wondered about the restrictions that would be put on her life. Kristi developed a meningococcal infection and died the next day, a tragedy that put us all in shock. Her death seemed so unfair! But Kristi had written an article about pain and suffering just days before her unexpected death. The Hermeiers shared it in a memorial letter that they sent at the beginning of Advent. In part it read:

"Who hasn't heard someone in desperation or grief ask the unanswerable 'why?' And who had the power and wisdom to respond? Once we accept that sometimes there are no answers, at least for now, we experience a release of those gnawing doubts, and become free to start learning."

I too could be freed. I too could learn.

A young friend from Koininia went to Cursillo and came back bubbling with enthusiasm. "I've been tickled by God," Karen giggled, and asked if I'd meet with her weekly to share

our spiritual growth and frustrations. I agreed, but I let
Karen do most of the sharing. I didn't want her to see how
much I still doubted God's love.

My toes began to itch. Little red dots spread and became
angry red blotches, and the somewhat petty annoyance took
on a nightmare quality. Dr. Smith thought it was a flare
symptom and upped my cortisone. That didn't help. The
burning itch intensified so that the only relief came from
soaking my feet in ice water.

Then Dr. Smith moved out of town and I had to find a
new doctor. The Hermeiers had nothing but praise for the
young man who had treated Kristi, so I decided to try him.
Dr. Josephson was extremely bright and had specialized in
lupus and related diseases in medical school. After putting me
in the hospital for tests he came to the conclusion that the
itching didn't indicate a flare at all; I had a rare inflammation
of the capillaries of my toes—something called erythro-
melalgia. It is too uncommon to have a definitive cure, and
we tried one medication after another without success. I
couldn't sleep without sleeping pills, and even with pills I
was waking up in the middle of the night hysterical from the
relentlessness of the itching. Tom would hold and soothe me,
but eventually he would fall asleep. I was wide awake. I didn't
think to pray. I cried and I felt very alone.

I told this to Karen one Saturday morning. I was tired and
cross, and my feet were sore from the continuous use of ice.
She opened her Bible to Psalm 56:8: "You have seen me
tossing and turning through the night. You have collected all
my tears and preserved them in your bottle! You have
recorded every one in your book."

"I've really been touched by that verse," she said
thoughtfully. "He's there collecting each and every tear . . . "

The verse seemed written just for me. At four A.M. when I
was crying and scratching in vain at my toes, God was there.
He didn't release me from my torment, but because he loves
me, he suffered too. My pain was his pain.

I thought back on the past years. I thought of all the physical and emotional and spiritual pain I had experienced. God had always been there hurting with me. He had been there when the pain of a flare kept me from walking. He was there when we canceled our adoption. He was there at Ro's funeral when I didn't even care if he existed.

Jensen's theology of the Cross came back, this time in three dimensions. Faith is most real when suffering keeps us from "feeling" God. Faith is strengthened in our weakness. But knowing that didn't keep me from waking up and crying with pain in the middle of the night. I still experienced despair, wondering if we'd ever find a medication that worked. But now there was an intangible sweetness and comfort in knowing that even as I cried, God was there crying with me. The deep darkness evaporated even in the midst of my depression. I was again walking in the sunshine.

One Sunday morning just before Valentine's Day I had just about decided to stay home from church and Sunday school. I had been awake most of the night with my itching toes, and the latest medication had left me with the side effect of a severe headache. I was down, and I just didn't feel like putting on my happy face and pretending that all was right in my world. I finally did go, probably from habit more than anything else, but I got nothing out of the church service. My toes and head hurt too much. I went on to the Koinonia Sunday school class and struggled to concentrate on the lesson. When it was over and we were all idly chattering, I decided on impulse to tell them of my pain. I told them how I cried in the night, how sore my skin was, and how the medications seemed to add to my problems rather than relieve them. I told them how hard it was for me to pray.

An awkward silence filled the room. I saw tears on some of their young faces, and I suddenly felt ashamed of burdening those dear people. I knew that they already were praying for me; what good did it do to force them to keep sharing in my problems? I made a feeble excuse and left early.

Tom told me we were going out to eat on Valentine's Day. At six P.M. the doorbell rang, and the Koinonians came bounding in, each carrying part of a feast they had planned for us. Pork roast, potatoes, vegetable casseroles. Salad, rolls, cherry pie. They put their dishes on the table, gave me a huge homemade card, and vanished before I could get my wits about me. It was their way of saying, "We may not be able to stop the itching, but we care."

The card is red and white and ruffled. In painstaking embroidery it says, "Smile, Edee, God loves you." I've hung the card in our bedroom because I want to be able to see it when my toes itch at four A.M. I want to see it when I'm tired and hurting. The card has become tangible evidence to me that Koinonia cares, and the fact that Koinonia cares is tangible evidence that God cares.

I no longer search for proof of God's love for me. The proof has been there all along. The nameless woman in the hospital chapel who challenged me to trust in that love was a reflection of his concern. So were the members of our congregations. The Bible camp staff who had held the prayer service. My friends from Cursillo. Lynn. Ro. Karen. My beloved Tom. All along God had been shining on me through the faces of the communion of saints.

Ps 56:8

TEN

Joy. Such a nebulous word. I sought after joy all my life and it always eluded me. Then, through physical pain and emotional blackness, joy found me.

When God promised me perpetual joy I mistakenly equated it with perpetual happiness, the shallow "ha-ha" kind of happiness that was a result of getting my own way. But that kind of happiness never lasts. The Lord himself admitted unhappiness to his disciples in Gethsemane.

"My soul is crushed with horror and sadness to the point of death," he said in Matthew 26:38. If Jesus himself could feel this way, surely I too could experience unhappiness without guilt, knowing that it is just a transitory feeling that has nothing to do with faith.

God revealed his true joy to me slowly and gently. Each time that I thought I understood it completely, he added another dimension. It was like the ever-widening rings of waves caused by a stone thrown into calm water.

There is, first of all, the vivid and bubbly joy that is a result of being "tickled by God," as my friend Karen says. That is a gift, an unexplainable spiritual high that we often refer to as a "mountain-top experience." It is very real. But although it strengthens and refreshes us, we cannot stay on the mountain top. Life is lived mostly in the valleys below. Joy can be this kind of high, but it is also more.

There is a kind of joy that is a grateful response to the bounty of God's blessings. It has little to do with the size of our blessings; it has everything to do with how we view them. Before my lupus was diagnosed I was discontented with my lot in life. Tom wasn't home enough; the children needed my every minute. I never was caught up on my housework, and I had no chance to develop as an individual. A few short weeks in the hospital showed me the bounty of having a loving husband and two healthy children. My work became my privilege. Joy can be a bone-deep contentment with our lot in life, but it is also more.

Joy is knowing that even our crosses in life can be used by God for his glory and for our good. We are too finite to see the overall picture, but we can trustingly thank him even for the pain in our life because we have the assurance that though he doesn't deliberately cause us pain, he is still there and in control. Joy is this reassurance, but it is also more.

Joy is a deep, soul-releasing knowledge that whatever our situation, God is hanging in there with us. He rejoices when we rejoice; he cries when we cry. He allows us our free will (even though he knows we will hurt ourselves by it) just because he loves us so much. He is always there. Emmanuel—God with us. As far as I know, this is ultimate joy. It is something that death and depression, doubt and lupus flares cannot weaken. Is there even more to joy than this? I do not know. I wonder and thrill at the possibilities.

I still have my shadows. I feel remote from God. I chafe at my continual fatigue and my inability to run and play with abandon in the summer sun. But step by step God guides me along, picking me up when I stumble, wiping away my tears of self-pity. God has put my hands in the hands of other Christians so that we may help each other along the way. Truly I walk in God's sunshine.

A delicious postscript. A few months ago Tom received a
call from Luther Seminary in Minneapolis telling him that he
had been accepted to work on an archeological dig in Israel
this summer. The next afternoon the mail brought me a
contract for this manuscript. Both of our dreams had become
reality in the space of twenty-four hours. God was not only
smiling on us, he was downright chuckling! No, he was
probably rolling with holy glee! Tom and I and the boys
jumped all over the furniture and screamed hosannas. Then
we gathered our friends at a local ice cream parlor for
monstrous celebration sundaes. We were giddy with
excitement; that evening there seemed to be no limit to what
we could accomplish.

We haven't had a chance yet, but soon we're going to sit
down as a family and dream some new dreams. We'll make
them even wilder this time around. We're learning,
sometimes the hard way, that with our loving God, nothing
is impossible.

Matt 26:38